PRAISE FOR *MEDIOCRITY*

"Taxpayers invest in schools to educate the rising generation—not subject them to ideological agendas and the political views of activist teachers. And yet, across the country, our institutions have been captured by those who want to shape the minds of our children. Don't dismiss this as a passing fad or a set of isolated incidents. *Mediocrity* explains how the dumbing down of schools has been methodical and intentional. Read this book to realize how bad things have become, then take action to allow your children to find a better way."

   —*Glenn Beck*, radio host and author

"Almost daily, videos emerge of activist teachers promoting their personal views and ideological agendas onto kids in K-12 classes across America. Many people are shocked and surprised by the videos I post, yet others remain dismissive, arguing that these are isolated incidents taken out of context. Not so, as Connor and Corey explain in this compelling and insightful book! *Mediocrity* serves up one example after another of the sad state of today's schools—not to depress you or make you feel defeated. To the contrary: information is power, and the sooner you can realize the scope of the problems we face, the sooner you'll be able to seek solutions. Read *Mediocrity* now!"

   —*Chaya Raichik*, creator, Libs of TikTok

"WARNING: Do not read this book unless you're ready to make big changes to save your kids or grandkids. *Mediocrity* is a must-read warning manual—and call to action to protect our kids from the insanity of today's government schools."

   —*Pete Hegseth*, co-host, Fox & Friends Weekend

"Every parent needs to read this book, which raises a warning voice about what's going on in today's schools. Connor and Corey have done excellent work highlighting the problems facing public education and provide parents with the analysis they need to make better decisions for their children. If you have kids, you need to read this book."

—*Christopher Rufo, senior fellow, Manhattan Institute*

"In an era in which human curiosity and creativity are more essential than ever, government schools are instead doubling-down on their push for conformity and compliance. In this must-read book, Connor and Corey expose the many harms of government schooling and urge parents to consider alternatives."

—*Kerry McDonald, senior education fellow, Foundation for Economic Education*

MEDIOCRITY

40 Ways Government Schools are Failing Today's Students

CONNOR BOYACK AND COREY DEANGELIS

LIBERTAS PRESS

SALT LAKE CITY, UT

Libertas Press
2183 W Main, Suite A102
Lehi, UT 84043

Mediocrity: 40 Ways Government Schools are Failing Today's Students — 1st ed.

ISBN-13 979-8-88688-008-3 (paperback)

For bulk orders, send inquiries to info@libertas.org.

10 9 8 7 6 5 4 3 2 1

CONTENTS

FOREWORD

Imagine with me you are watching the next Olympic Games. American athletes are competing in all the usual events, but instead of breaking records and leading the medal count, no US athlete ever makes the podium. The stars and stripes never raised. The national anthem never played.

You would be appalled, right? Social media would be ablaze: "Impossible!" "Horrible!" "Not acceptable!" Commentators, fans, and athletes would demand changes and improvements by the next games. There would be a sense of national disappointment from family dining room tables to board rooms. America competes to *win*. We do not accept mediocrity.

Now apply that hypothetical to education. For decades, America's government schools have lagged the rest of the world. We are not in the top ten in *any* subject—in fact, far from it. And the gap isn't closing. There has been painfully little progress made to improve student achievement, and generations of American students have suffered the consequences.[1]

That stubborn fact is one of many reasons I have long advocated for a transformational change in how we approach education in our country. Doing so hasn't won me a lot of fans among the education establishment. While I served as the eleventh secretary for the United States Department of Education (a federal agency that does not and cannot serve its intended purpose and consequently should not exist), I constantly battled against entrenched interests that sought to protect the status quo, their power, and their jobs. As I tried to empower parents by removing government burdens, one of the largest teachers' unions excoriated me for supposedly waging "a full-blown crusade" against students that "put the future of public education... at risk."

I may have put their power at risk, but public education—and more importantly, the students and families who expect public education to live up to its mission—has been at risk for a long, long time.

Just consider Augusta Fells Savage Institute of Visual Arts, a government high school in Baltimore. There, Tiffany France was expecting her 17-year-old son to graduate in May 2021, only to learn his GPA was 0.13. You read that right—zero point one three. Even more jaw-dropping, he was ranked near the top half of his class. The school had 434 students enrolled, and only two of them tested proficient in math and English. As Tiffany said: "[The schools] need a whole lot of help. These kids aren't prepared for life, they're just not."[2] It's hard to argue it was about a lack of funding. At more than $17,000 per student per year, Baltimore's school funding is in the top ten nationally, yet 41 percent of the city's high schoolers have a GPA below 1.0.[3]

These results seem shocking, but they are not uncommon. According to the most recent Nation's Report Card, only 31 percent of America's eighth graders are proficient in reading. Thirty percent are "below basic" readers—functionally illiterate. And only 27 percent of eighth graders are proficient in math—an abysmally failing grade. It's not a question of funding. The United States spends more than $750 billion on K-12 government schools each year.[4] That translates, on average, to more than $15,000 per student, which ranks as nearly the highest spending country in the world.[5] In some places, like New York or D.C., it's upward of $30,000 per student.

Given the abysmal outcomes, it's little wonder that one in three college students are required to take some form of remedial course. That number jumps to two in three at community colleges.[6] These are students who have been admitted to and enrolled in college, yet they are paying to learn material they were supposed to have learned in high school... or earlier.

Perhaps worse yet, one in four young people who want to serve in the military can't pass the military's basic skills test,[7] forcing the Army to create its own remedial program for recruits.[8] Yes, you as a taxpayer are paying for our government's military to fix the failure of our government's schools—which you also pay for. Instead of spending time and resources preparing soldiers to protect our nation, they are teaching information that recruits should have learned in school.

Forty years after the warning bells were first sounded, we are still a "Nation at Risk." Arguably, one even more at risk today.

For many of America's families, the COVID-19 shutdowns made this tangible, clear, and acutely pressing in a way it never had before. The abject failures of the government-run, union-controlled education system have been laid bare for <u>all</u> to see. Many families awakened to the reality that their school system doesn't always—or ever—have the best interests of their children in mind. And perhaps you feel that this is a new phenomenon in America—a sudden decline in the quality of schools.

But the mediocrity we see in government schools was, in fact, always the design. The father of America's government-run education system, Horace Mann, once wrote that parents should be viewed as having given their children as "hostages to our cause."

You read that right: hostages. The stark truth is that America's students are held hostage to a system that assigns them to a school, teaches them what it wants, and does its best to keep families out of the conversation. As I describe in my book, *Hostages No More*, we must take action to ensure our children, our families, and our teachers are no longer hostage to a broken, one-size-fits-all system. We cannot continue to offer the same education in the same schools and expect improved results. We must fundamentally rethink our approach to education, and importantly, restructure the power balance to put the needs of students above the desires of "the system."

I've long advocated for education freedom, the idea that students should be free to learn wherever, whenever, and however works best for them. That includes freedom from forced indoctrination. Our kids deserve to have their minds challenged and horizons expanded, not their perspectives narrowed by the political preferences of the adults who run their schools.

But in order to understand education freedom and how it will solve the problems that have persistently beset America's government-run, union-controlled education system, we need to fully understand the magnitude of the problem we confront. That's where this book comes in.

Connor Boyack and Corey DeAngelis have put together a compelling review of the problems with government schools that is sure to wake parents up to the disastrous status quo too many people still accept as normal. *Mediocrity* is a call to arms. It couldn't have come at a better time. Parents and grandparents need to read it and join us in the fight to rescue more children from the tyranny of low expectations and inexcusable results.

I hope you'll join Connor, Corey, me and millions of students, teachers, families and leaders who support the education freedom effort. Reading this book is your next step on that journey. Be prepared to be shocked and angered by what you read in the pages that follow. And note that these chapters are not 40 outlier examples; they are like 40 puzzle pieces that, when put together, allow you to see the full picture of the problem. The government school system has failed students, families, and our nation for far too long. Understanding the true breadth and depth of the problem is the first step toward joining together to solve it.

Betsy DeVos
January 2023

AUTHOR'S NOTE

Why use the term "government schools"? These taxpayer-funded institutions have had many names over the decades, as this book describes—common schools, factory schools, neighborhood schools, and public schools. But throughout this book, we have opted to refer to them in a more direct manner, free from any flowery descriptors that may mask this relationship.

The government created, controls, operates, and funds these schools. They exist only with the blessing and support of the government. They are inherently part of the political process and, thus, subject to the same corruption, inefficiency, and bureaucratic mismanagement that is seen elsewhere in government.

We wish to be forthright with our readers, and so we have chosen to refer to them throughout *Mediocrity* as government schools.

INTRODUCTION

A recently-formed group called the National Commission on Excellence in Education took up the charge to review America's schools to see how well (or how *poorly*) they were doing. The Commission's members held over two dozen meetings across the country to hear from administrators, teachers, scholars, and students. They reviewed data from education experts and letters from concerned citizens. After eighteen months of review, they released their report.

Let's pause for just a moment. If you had the opportunity to review how education in the twenty-first century is working in our country, what might you conclude? Let's see if what this group recently said resonates with you.

Here's a small excerpt from their thirty-six-page report—what they called "An Open Letter to the American People":

> The educational foundations of our society are presently being eroded by a rising tide of mediocrity that threatens our very future as a nation and a people.

> If an unfriendly foreign power had attempted to impose on America the mediocre educational performance that exists today, we might well have viewed it as an act of war. As it stands, we have allowed this to happen to ourselves.[1]

Strong words, right? But think of what is going on today: test scores are declining, school libraries are full of questionable books while lacking others, teachers often push an agenda, and school board members resort to calling parents potential domestic terrorists for passionately pushing back against them in public meetings. When you consider the current state of the education landscape in America, it's fair to say that the "educational foundations of our society are presently being eroded by a rising tide of mediocrity." The evidence is abundant, as this book aims to show.

But before continuing, we need to make a quick confession.

This Commission was not *recently* formed, as we led you to believe. In fact, it was convened four decades ago. Ronald Reagan's administration oversaw its work, and the report, titled *A Nation at Risk*, was published on April 26, 1983—exactly forty years to the day from the publication date of this book.

It was 14,610 days ago—even longer, depending on when you're reading this book—that America was warned about this rising tide of mediocrity that "threatens our very future as a nation and a people." Now, we invite you to consider how things have changed during that time. Do you think America's schools and the education landscape have materially improved? Has the tide of mediocrity receded? Has our society made significant strides in helping today's youth excel compared to a generation or two ago?

The questions answer themselves. But if you're not convinced about that, reading this book will persuade you otherwise.

Mediocrity is not a book about solutions to these problems. Those solutions exist, and we will unabashedly declare here at the outset that we support so-called "school choice" that disrupts the schooling monopoly and creates a competitive landscape so that quality will increase and prices will decrease. Parents should be empowered to pursue education solutions that best support their children. Much has been written about this topic, and abundant evidence exists to back it up.[2]

Instead, this book focuses on the problems themselves. Despite a general recognition that America's schools are in a sad state, too many parents and grandparents are unaware of just how pervasive the problems are. They may be concerned about the rising tide of mediocrity but unaware just how badly the educational foundations have eroded in recent years. They bring their bias—*I went to public school and I turned out fine!*—and, thus, continue treading water as the tide level surges around their family. Without warnings to realize how bad things are today, these adults will often passively accept the soft bigotry of low expectations.

Those warnings can save lives. Consider the story of twenty-year-old Brandon Schmidt, who was playing in the water at Lake Michigan in late 2018. There were no signs advising against swimming and no lifeguards around in a lake featuring "riptide and longshore tides [that] are unparalleled when it comes to danger among all the Great Lakes."[3] That year, there were 117 reported drownings in the Great Lakes[4]—and Brandon became one of them, unable to combat the strong currents that engulfed him. His mother later reported, "A couple deputies and the sheriff responded, but no one was capable of getting in that water... because nobody was water-safety trained."[5] Had Brandon realized the danger he was getting himself into, he might have changed his behavior.

Consider this book a warning sign about the tide of mediocrity that has risen far higher than when *A Nation at Risk* was published forty years ago. The purpose is not to make you feel angry or incapable of tackling the massive problems that pervade government schools in America. Like a good warning sign, the purpose is to encourage you to *change your behavior*.

One definition of insanity is to do the same thing over and over and expect different results. Tens of millions of kids attend government schools each year and are taught from increasingly dumbed-down curricula—with a heavy focus on becoming "college and career ready," despite the fact that more remedial courses in college are being offered than ever before[6] and today's schools train kids for last century's careers.[7] Children are increasingly unprepared for a changing world, barely treading water amid the tide of mediocrity that threatens them. It's insane to keep doing what we've been doing and expect that the tide won't continue to rise.

With forty years now having passed since *A Nation at Risk* warned the American people about this societal threat, let's review forty ways government schools are failing our children.

SHUTTERED SCHOOLS, SLIPPING TEST SCORES

It may seem pedantic to point out, but "public" schools are government schools, which are operated and controlled by... the government. Supporters often like to call these institutions "neighborhood" schools to downplay this aspect, but they can't hide the truth—and the truth became especially clear during the COVID-19 pandemic when government officials across the country in both major political parties shut down their schools and sent kids home.

The results weren't great.

Juggling Zoom school and start-and-stop schedules with kids going home and then back to school and then back home again appears to have made an impact on performance. That's at least according to the "nation's report card"—the National Assessment of Educational Progress (NAEP). This congressionally mandated, bi-annual review of academic progress shows long-term math performance dropping for the first time. Just 26 percent of eighth graders now perform math proficiently, down from 33 percent in 2019. And reading scores saw their biggest drop in three decades, falling back to 1992 levels when the first reading test was used.[1] Thirty-three percent of fourth graders were reading at a proficient level in 2022, down from 35 percent in 2019. Eighth graders declined from 34 percent to 31 percent. You read that right: fewer than one-third of eighth graders in America can read proficiently. Mediocrity indeed.

Even worse, the biggest declines were seen in lower performing students, thus increasing the gap between high and low performers. (In other words, successful students weathered the challenges well enough, while those struggling were left to struggle even more.) More children with disabilities or English-language learners tested below "proficiency" than before they were banished from school campuses.

Peggy Carr, commissioner of the National Center for Education Statistics, said, "It's clear that COVID-19 shocked American education and stunned the academic growth of this age group of students. We don't make this statement lightly."[2] But she's not quite correct—it wasn't a virus that caused this decline. This was the result of how government officials responded to the virus and made unilateral decrees that had significant effects on student performance.

Of course, NAEP scores are only a data point; test scores are a sometimes useful metric to assess knowledge and comprehension. But they are not perfect, and we shouldn't consider them to be an accurate reflection of student achievement and learning comprehension. The NAEP itself has changed over time, once tracking progress in over twenty areas before being reduced down to a smaller number.[3] Congress has tweaked what is tracked and pushed changes that, to some, have represented "an abandonment of fundamental principles and the creation of a testing enterprise that [does] more harm than good."[4] Critics allege that it emphasizes "psychometric efficiency and uniformity over meaningfulness and improvement of student learning."[5] In other words, it's an effective tool for school bureaucrats to implement in a standardized fashion across a large group of kids... but it's not exactly useful for measuring actual learning and progress. And the release of NAEP scores is always accompanied by government officials claiming we need more and better testing with more and better instructions—more and better of what has been done before. In the words of Natalie Wexler, author of *The Knowledge Gap*, "It's as though we've been prescribing medicine that is actually toxic—and when the patient fails to improve, or even gets worse, we just call for larger doses."[6] There's that idea of insanity popping up again.

Test scores are also problematic because they are not always indicative of what is actually happening. To some, tests like the NAEP are "like trying to measure the progress of a basketball game by measuring how far one player moves in three steps. It tells us nearly nothing about what's actually happening or what is likely to happen."[7] But the data is interesting, at least, in comparing performance—in this case, pre- and post-pandemic. To see such a marked decline in test scores in such a short amount of time is significant and revealing.

Yet the insanity continues—the idea of doing what has been done in the past and thinking that the mediocrity will abate. Government school proponents concede that the low test scores are concerning but continue to stress the importance of doubling down on what has been done before. We're told that "state policy leaders must continue the funding necessary to enable students to make up lost ground."[8] But money doesn't equate to improved education outcomes—indeed, some of the worst performing school districts receive the most money. In 2013, American taxpayers spent on average $11,791 per student and six years later averaged $13,187—yet NAEP outcomes were flat or declining. As one economist said, "It's a stretch to think that when new funding goes only to sports fields, for instance, or toward paying for retirement promises for former school employees, that such spending choices are likely to boost reading scores."[9] More funding of a bureaucracy doesn't directly correlate to better student outcomes.

Let's imagine for a moment that this decline in test scores didn't actually happen. Think of a world in which the NAEP scores instead continued to rise and rise. Would this be a self-congratulatory moment to suggest that the tide of mediocrity is receding? One author argues that *A Nation at Risk* was misguided and should have instead described a "rising tide of test scores,"[10] since the Iowa Test of Basic Skills, for example, had reached their highest score level compared to previous years. In a world where many educators "teach to the test" and students prepare by memorizing and practicing test taking, should improving test scores even excite us? Do parents feel like their children are receiving a well-rounded, quality education simply because the nation's "report card" showed a minor uptick in proficiency?

The government's cruel response in managing its schools during and after COVID-19 set back the educational progress of many students. "Two weeks to slow the spread" became two years to increase mediocrity for millions of students. Parents need to demand better.

READING, WRITING, AND...
GENDER IDENTITY?

The foundation of modern education has long rested upon the "three Rs": reading, writing, and arithmetic. These basic aspects of pedagogy are the core of helping children attain educational competence. And yet, the times they are a-changin'.

Across America, teachers are increasingly creating so-called safe spaces for discussions around sexual orientation and gender identity. Despite 70 percent of Americans opposing the idea,[1] teachers like Lori Caldeira actively court children into LGBTQ clubs without parental knowledge or consent. "Sometimes we don't really want to keep records because if parents get upset that their kids are coming?" she rhetorically said. "We're like, 'Yeah, I don't know. Maybe they came?' You know, we would never want a kid to get in trouble for attending if their parents are upset." Caldeira has separately and publicly stated that, regarding the sexual topics she discusses with minors, "What happens in this room, stays in this room."[2]

She's certainly not an anomaly. Seven states require that teachers discuss LGBTQ topics, and the federal government "recommends that schools include gender identity in their sex education programs."[3] In many states, such as Washington,[4] Ohio,[5] and Maryland,[6] teachers are advised to withhold information from parents about gender identity discussions and decisions made by their children at school. "The schools are willing to hide from parents that their children are making life-altering decisions," an attorney representing concerned parents said, "cutting those children off from the care and counsel of those who know them best."[7]

But these decisions made by students about their gender and preferred pronouns don't happen in a vacuum. The clubs hosted by Caldeira and her peers across the country actively promote a culture of gender dysphoria, leading impressionable children to be confused about their identity and development. One California parent, Jessica Konen, sued two of her child's teachers, alleging they manipulated her daughter into changing her gender identity under pressure (or what some might call "grooming"). Konen claims "the two teachers actively sought out students who they thought were struggling with their identities and invited them to the school's Equality Club" where they would "coach students on LGBT+ identities, such as homosexuality, bisexuality, transgenderism, gender non-conformity, etc., and how to express those identities."[8] And the children had homework, too. The teachers "would instruct students to research a particular topic and then have follow up discussions with the student about that research."

In some schools, the three Rs aren't what you might expect them to be. Consider the kindergarten teacher in Massachusetts who uses "Rights, Respect, Responsibility"—a sex education curriculum "that fully meets the National Sexuality Education Standards and seeks to address both the functional knowledge related to sexuality and the specific skills necessary to adopt healthy behaviors."[9] For kindergarten students, this teacher adapts the curriculum to introduce "the idea of gender as part of an exploration of identity." The teacher "explains that people use all sorts of pronouns: he, she, they, ze. He introduces the terms transgender and gender queer but doesn't fully define them because that is too much for kindergartners..."[10]

Teachers are using clubs as a means to engage children in a discussion about their sexual orientation. In over four thousand schools, GSA clubs operate with teacher and student participation. Initially, these were Gay-Straight Alliances—an opportunity to help homosexual students feel welcome and find friends. In 2016, they rebranded as Gender and Sexuality Alliances under the purview of their parent organization, GSA Network.[11] Children are heavily propagandized with rival gender theory—for example, "allies" are told to do "the self and collective work to analyze how we contribute to the oppression of Trans, Queer, Non-binary/Gender Non-Conforming, Black, Indigenous, youth of color."[12] Beyond that, they are encouraged to "commit to dismantling these systems for collective liberation."[13] This sounds like Marxist brainwashing, not quality education grounded in science and rationality.

Like the Fight Club, teachers are trained not to talk about these clubs and what goes on in them. Even elementary school teachers actively promote cultivating the curiosity of impressionable children by reading stories and watching videos "about all different genders" to prompt questions to "come up organically," which then serves as a recruitment opportunity for club discussion where they can talk "really explicitly and seriously about sexuality and gender."[14] These clubs don't always require parental consent; one teacher pointed out that her school does not require permission slips since their club meets during school hours. Another teacher said that they had to obtain permission, but he simply said the club was about "inclusivity."[15]

What was once a goodwill gesture of homosexual and heterosexual children befriending one another has now been co-opted into a breeding ground for radical left-wing teachers to promote gender discussion and dysphoria among highly impressionable children, even at very young ages, without their parents having any knowledge about or say in the matter. Seventy-one percent of registered voters are "extremely or very concerned about what's being taught in public schools,"[16] and with each new day bringing more revelations about what is going on inside the closed classroom doors of government schools across America, that number—like the tide of mediocrity—is sure to increase.

POOR PREPARATION FOR GRADUATES

Eight thousand students first took the Scholastic Aptitude Test (SAT) when it launched in 1926.[1] Within three decades, half a million high school seniors were taking the test each year. But this exam was geared more toward Ivy League schools and other selective universities, prompting Dr. Everett Lindquist in 1958 to suggest a second type of test for students interested in attending less prestigious colleges. He was no random bystander—Dr. Lindquist was part of the group that administered the SAT. His peers rejected the idea, so he launched the American College Test (ACT).[2]

In the words of the *New York Times*, "The ACT has long been like Pepsi to the SAT's Coke."[3] With an average of over 1.5 million students taking the ACT each year over the past decade,[4] it has become a ubiquitous method of assessing the knowledge and competence of high school seniors across America. And the results? Well, they're not that great.

The ACT has four sections: reading, math, English, and science. Points range from 1 to 36—with 36 being the highest score—and the final "composite score" is the rounded average of those four numbers. For the past decade, the average ACT score has consistently hovered just above 21.[5] In the past few years, even before the COVID-19 pandemic, that nationwide average dipped below 21 and continued declining. The average score in 2022 was 19.8—a failing grade at 55 percent of the total points possible.

What does this trend mean? One of the ACT's executive staff explains that "The score decline really reflects students' lack of access to a rigorous high school curriculum."[6] And while the pandemic-related problems often bring focused attention to an acute decline in educational performance, "this is part of a trend that... has been happening for a long time."[7] In other words, America's high school graduates—after a decade of heavy instruction, testing, and regimented curriculum mandates—are failing.

The implication here is that most students are not academically prepared for higher education despite all the K-12 instruction they've received. These consistently low scores "draw attention to the fundamental flaws at the core of many of America's government-run schools." Fundamental. Core. These are not superficial outcomes that might shift anytime soon based on fleet- ing circumstances. They demonstrate, rather, that the "educational foundations of our society [have been] eroded by a rising tide of mediocrity."[8] What else would you call what is effectively a 55 percent grade when measuring the outcomes of a decade plus of gov- ernment schooling?

Another way to analyze the data from the most re- cent ACT report[9] is looking at each subject separately. Perhaps, we might theorize, the broad average is hiding some good news? Maybe America's students are fail- ing at science and math but excelling at reading and English, or some other combination of the sort? The ACT has developed College Readiness Benchmarks— minimum scores in each of the subjects which are "sta- tistically correlated with success in freshman-level col- lege courses."[10] In other words, students would need to reach that particular score or higher to have a likely chance of doing well in that topic in college. As one example, a student would need to achieve a minimum score of 22 in math to do well in college algebra. As of 2022, only 22 percent of students met all four mini- mum benchmarks in all four subjects. And here's what is worse: despite 80 percent of parents feeling confi- dent that their high school graduate children will be "well prepared" for success in college,[11] a staggering 42 percent of students scored below the minimum level needed for all four benchmarks.[12]

The CEO of the ACT organization, Janet Goodwin, noted that this was "the fifth consecutive year of declines in average scores, a worrisome trend that began long before the disruption of the COVID-19 pandemic, and has persisted."[13] While some educators simply strive for returning to pre-pandemic levels to erase the setbacks we've seen, Goodwin believes that this "would be insufficient and a disservice to students and educators." Why? Because of what Goodwin called "systemic failures" that are "an urgent national priority and imperative."[14] Her language seems to suggest that the authors of *A Nation at Risk* weren't misguided in their open letter to the American people four decades ago. But insanity prevails, and in recent decades we've seen school administrators and curriculum creators continue to do more of the same, hoping for improvement. It hasn't happened. It won't happen.

Of course, standardized tests like the SAT and ACT only go so far—and their usefulness may be on the decline as more colleges drop the admissions requirement to take such a test.[15] But the underlying reality is something we still need to confront: is the government's K-12 system of student instruction adequately educating children and preparing them for higher education, careers, or life? If one assumes that tests like the ACT are at least a helpful method of assessing the quality of output such schools are producing, then we must conclude that today's schools are sub-mediocre— they are, on the whole, and especially for low-income and rural students, poorly preparing them to be competent graduates.

PASSIONATE PARENTS ARE DOMESTIC TERRORISTS?

Research confirms what we all implicitly understand to be true: more parent engagement in a child's school experience leads to improved educational outcomes.[1] The more involved a parent is, the better their child will do educationally. For decades, many teachers have bemoaned how disconnected and uninvolved their students' parents were in the education process. In 1988, just five years after *A Nation at Risk* was published, the Carnegie Foundation for the Advancement of Teaching surveyed 22,000 teachers and "found a sense of frustration in the classroom, both over 'the lack of support they receive from parents' and over a feeling of 'powerlessness in teaching.'"[2] A full 90 percent of polled teachers indicated that "lack of parental support was a problem at their schools."[3] More recently, almost half of all teachers asked about parent engagement in a 2018 survey indicated that many of their students' parents were "hard to reach and engage."[4]

Despite many teachers desiring more parent engagement, not all of them feel that way. As Zoom school emerged during COVID-19—the video-enabled remote instruction as schools were shut down—many parents suddenly had easy access to review what was being taught to their children, and by whom. One teacher in Philadelphia publicly voiced frustration that "We'll never be quite sure who is overhearing the discourse" between him and his students, and wondered, "How much have students depended on the (somewhat) secure barriers of our physical classrooms to encourage vulnerability? How many of us have installed some version of 'what happens here stays here' to help this?"[5] And he made clear his concern that parents would interfere with his propaganda efforts: "If we are engaged in the messy work of destabilizing a kids [sic] racism or homophobia or transphobia—how much do we want their classmates' parents piling on?"

It was precisely this greater transparency into government schools that prompted many parents to begin speaking out and voicing their concerns—engaging in the very process that many teachers were long frustrated wasn't happening. Whether due to questionable curriculum content, school shutdowns, activist teachers, or mask mandates, parents across the country began attending school board meetings in droves to observe, complain, and demand action. One might expect this to be a welcome engagement of concerned citizens, but many elected officials instead construed this behavior as "micro-aggressions" worthy of their derision and attack. For example, on May 18, 2021, the Scottsdale Unified Governing Board canceled its meeting because of what they called "a belligerent mob," or what others might call parents hoping to speak out and be heard about mask mandates and Critical Race Theory. Amy Carney, a local parent, later said that "while she had never attended a school board meeting before, the pandemic opened up many parents' eyes to what is happening in schools and what is not happening in schools."[6]

Later that year, as political pressure was applied at school boards across the country, the National School Boards Association, which represents 90,000 school board members, wrote a letter to President Biden claiming that "America's public schools and its education leaders are under an immediate threat." That threat was not the "rising tide of mediocrity" warned about decades prior. In the view of this organization comprised of elected officials, the threat was alleged "threats of violence and acts of intimidation" from outspoken parents. The group asked for FBI involvement along with support from a variety of other federal agencies since "the classification of these heinous actions could be the equivalent to a form of domestic terrorism and hate crimes" and potentially in violation of the PATRIOT Act, among other laws.[7]

It was only later revealed that the Association had been colluding on this letter directly with the White House for weeks prior to its release.[8] An earlier draft of the letter called for the "Army National Guard and its Military Police" to be deployed to protect school board members and called critical parents "plotters who are targeting schools and educators."[9] Less than a week later, in response to what he characterized as "a disturbing spike in harassment, intimidation, and threats of violence against school administrators, board members, teachers, and staff," U.S. Attorney General Merrick Garland issued a memo directing the FBI to investigate and to maintain "open dedicated lines of communication for threat reporting, assessment, and response."[10]

The backlash was swift. After significant pushback from parents and attention from the media, the National School Boards Association withdrew their letter and issued an apology, saying, "We regret and apologize for the letter" and "There was no justification for some of the language included."[11] But the damage had been done. After eight decades of existence, the organization is imploding and at risk of total collapse. Within months of the letter, nineteen states had withdrawn from the group or promised to when their annual membership expired.[12]

This entire affair calls into question to what degree teachers actually want parents involved. If that involvement is constrained to a tiny range of acceptable input, then when parents scrutinize things outside of that range or demand change, teachers may likely become defensive and perceive the pushback as "harassment" or "intimidation" as Merrick's memo suggested. But if internal reforms and tweaking at the edges of curriculum design or classroom management have not produced outcomes sufficient to pull the system out of its descent into mediocrity, external pressure may be needed. Such pressure is rarely welcomed by those who are part of the problem.

BROKEN OR WORKING AS INTENDED?

Many parents feel that the school system is broken—across America, teachers and textbooks are pushing an agenda and filling children's minds with information and ideas that are controversial or counterproductive to the healthy development of the children. They have in mind an idea of how schools ought to operate and see them falling far short. Consequently, they believe that the system is malfunctioning and simply needs to be fixed. Is this true?

That question can't be answered properly without understanding the original plans and purposes for which the system was created. Imagine, for example, that you're in a submarine. You hear some creaking in the pipes near you. Down the corridor, you see some steam emitting from an open valve. Above you there are gauges that show really high internal pressure inside of a row of tanks. Is any of this normal? The sounds are scary and seem to suggest there's a problem. But until you look at the original schematics and understand how the system was designed, it would be hard to know whether it was broken or working as intended.

The schematics of today's government schools were first designed in the mid-nineteenth century with heavy contributions from Horace Mann, one of the leading education reformers in America. He was an admirer of the schooling system being developed in Prussia, featuring a standardized curriculum, widespread testing, compulsory attendance, professionalization of teachers, and career training. It was an authoritarian, top-down model that emphasized the collective over the individual. Following a trip abroad to see this system in action for himself, Mann became a strong advocate for its implementation in America.

His lobbying effort was swift and successful. Mann was instrumental in getting Massachusetts to adopt the Prussian model of education statewide in 1852, and other states soon followed. What emerged in the years ahead was a new kind of school called the "factory model school," where both the design of the school building and the processes used within it were modeled after an actual factory. It was a linear system, moving students through standardized information, regulated processes, and grade levels by age—akin to a conveyor-belt process in a factory.

Mann's quest to industrialize education set up a framework—the foundations of a system—that other education reformers were then able to use to indoctrinate millions of children. Among others we might mention, John Dewey certainly takes the lead. A secular humanist who theorized an atheist utopia, Dewey stated the following in his book *My Pedagogic Creed*:

> I believe that every teacher should realize the dignity of his calling; that he is a social servant set apart for the maintenance of proper social order and the securing of the right social growth. I believe that in this way the teacher always is the prophet of the true God and the usherer in of the true kingdom of God.[1]

Dewey's "true kingdom of God" was government. The schooling system that was still being built across the country enabled Dewey and his like-minded reformers to, in Dewey's own words, "build up forces... whose natural effect is to undermine the importance and uniqueness of family life."[2] Academics were secondary; social transformation was the key, and families stood in the way. The "importance of public schools" facilitated, for Dewey and his allies, "the relaxation of older family ties."[3] The fundamental intent was to weaken a child's family relationships and strengthen his or her relationship to—and dependence upon—the state. As one prominent official in the National Education Association said in 1934, "The major function of the school is the social orientation of the individual. It must seek to give him understanding of the transition to a new social order."[4]

It might be tempting to dismiss the delusions of these early school architects as antiquated and irrelevant to our modern day. Surely the kind teachers at the nearby elementary school working hard to help our children don't share this goal to socially engineer the rising generation, right? This is no doubt true of many hardworking teachers who signed up to help kids reach their potential. But doing this within the modern school system is like growing tomatoes by planting seedlings in a small pot. The system's constraint—the size of the pot—limits the potential and shapes the future of the seedling. Because root development is limited by the confines of the small pot, the future outcomes of the plant—the size and quality of its fruit—are substantially restricted.

The person tending to that pot might be the sweetest person doing the best they know how. They might nurture the tender plant to the best of their ability, but their constant care can't compensate for the constraints imposed by the system. Only uprooting the plant and placing it in a different, larger pot will allow the caring gardener's efforts to be fully maximized. Similarly, good teachers aspiring to help students achieve their potential can only do so much in a system that constrains their growth with the Prussian-style, authoritarian "factory model" built for an economy that no longer exists. The best option for many students might be to place them in a different system altogether.

FLUSH WITH CASH AND FLUSHING CASH

Do you remember being graded on a curve in school? As students, we often welcomed this approach to learning because it was much easier. We didn't have to excel and achieve proficiency; we just needed to not do as poorly as our peers. This relative scoring measures you against others, rather than an objective standard. Let's run with this for a moment and see how America's schools stack up compared to other countries.

During the 1960s, scholars designed a methodology by which educational systems in different countries could be compared to one another. This ultimately led to the creation of the International Association for the Evaluation of Educational Achievement, which in 1967 conducted the first large-scale international study to assess how well students in twelve leading countries fared in mathematics.[1] The United States of America came in eleventh place out of twelve—Germany, France, Japan, England, and others all scored higher.

As the *Washington Post* wrote at the time, the United States' "poor showing... did not surprise the experts" because "teachers here are not as well trained, and that neither American students nor the society at large places as much value on mathematics achievement as do many countries abroad."[2]

Of course, that has since changed. Schools have been heavily pushing STEM subjects—science, technology, engineering, and math—with "increasing attention over the past decade with calls both for greater emphasis on these fields and for improvements in the quality of curricula and instruction."[3] Since the absurdly-named No Child Left Behind was passed in 2001, the federal government has required regular testing in math, giving it greater attention even in elementary school.[4] And most states require at least two years of courses just in that subject.[5] Suffice it to say, there's been a lot of attention on the topic throughout K-12 education. Has it been enough to pull the country's scores out of its comparative mediocrity?

In a word, no. The international academic rankings by the Programme for International Student Assessment (PISA) evaluate fifteen-year-olds in seventy-nine different countries to create a comparative score. The latest rankings place the US thirty-sixth among these countries in math with mediocre scores in the other tested subjects. This performance has remained fairly consistent since the first PISA assessment in 2000.[6] As one education researcher noted, "What surprises me is how stable US performance is. The scores have *always* been mediocre."[7] Compared only against the United States' largest economic competitors, the country ranks dead last.[8]

Surely investing more resources will help, right? Wrong. As of 2018, American taxpayers were compelled to spend an average of $14,400 for every student in elementary and secondary education, an amount that is 34 percent higher than the average spent by other countries in the PISA assessment.[9] (The amount spent on American students for higher education is $35,100—double the average of other countries.) More money does not equate to better performance. To back up that point further, consider the recent trend of education spending in the United States alone. Since 1970, "the inflation-adjusted cost of sending a student all the way through the K-12 system has almost tripled while test scores near the end of high school remain largely unchanged. Put another way, per-pupil spending and achievement are not obviously correlated."[10] Indeed, while standardized test scores have remained mostly flat or have declined, spending has skyrocketed.

The money definitely isn't going toward hiring more or better teachers. Despite the massive increase in spending on a per-student basis in recent decades, average teacher salaries have only increased by 8 percent during that entire time.[11] Since 2000, there has been an approximate 8 percent increase in the number of students and teachers—but a 37 percent increase in principals and assistant principals and an 88 percent increase in administrative staff.[12] American taxpayers now spend a sum exceeding a trillion dollars on schooling.[13] The K-12 school system is flush with cash and flushing cash.

And the number keeps going up as education outcomes continue to go down. While $14,400 was spent on average per student in 2018, as of 2020 that amount has increased to $16,000.[14] (Keep in mind that this is the average; in some areas, government schools spend well over $30,000 per student.[15]) And in the wake of COVID-19 bailouts pumping nearly $200 billion into the school system, that number is likely far higher.[16]

The school system is bloated with employed adults whose activities have little to no impact on educational outcomes of students. This problem is often made worse when considering how difficult it sometimes is to fire bad teachers. In 2015, the New York State School Boards Association reported that firing a teacher takes on average 830 days and costs $313,000—that is students being "taught" for over two school years by an adult who shouldn't be a teacher.[17] In New York City proper, over the course of an entire decade, the largest school district in the country fired only a dozen teachers due to incompetence.[18] The problems continue:

> Some teachers who can't be fired due to the highly restrictive teacher union contracts are assigned to "Temporary Reassignment Centers." In 2009, more than 600 New York City teachers reported to the Temporary Reassignment Centers dubbed "Rubber Rooms." Important to note, these "teachers" received their full salary as well as retirement contributions and accumulation of seniority.[19]

Here's the takeaway: the public school system has become more of a jobs program for adults than an education initiative for children.

SCHOOLS: A JOBS PROGRAM FOR ADULTS

Let's unpack this one a little more.

When Elon Musk took over Twitter in 2022, he immediately fired around half of the workforce—some 7,500 employees were on the payroll when his purchase was complete. Around 1,500 of these individuals were content moderators.[1] The mass layoffs were instituted, according to a company-wide memo, in order to "place Twitter on a healthy path."[2] In the year prior to the acquisition, the company generated some $5 billion in total revenue, yet was not profitable; the company ultimately lost $221 million, ending in the red. Toward the end of that year, Twitter had $182 million in net income for the fourth quarter, down from $222 million. But they spent $1.4 billion, a 35 percent increase over the prior period.[3]

That bloodletting isn't sustainable, of course. Musk's decision to reduce expenses was seen as a necessity. When asked, "Elon, what's the one thing that's most messed up at Twitter right now??" by a follower on Twitter (of course), he replied, "There seem to be 10 people 'managing' for every one person coding."[4] Hence the layoffs. By removing all the administrative cruft that had caked on top of the productive engineers and developers, Musk can reduce costs, better reward higher performers, and ensure that employees are directly servicing the product rather than operating multiple layers away from the customers they serve.

Government schools are experiencing an administrative bloat like Twitter was. Despite teacher pay stagnating (made even worse in light of heavy inflation reducing the purchasing power of their earnings), the amount of school budget being allocated to administrators has ballooned unbelievably. "Half of the states now have more non-instructional personnel than teachers."[5] From 1950 to 2012, enrollment of school students had increased 96 percent while teacher growth was 252 percent and non-teaching school administrators grew 702 percent. This "rise in non-teaching staff was more than seven times faster than the increase in students."[6]

Like unproductive Twitter managers, these school administrators are paid well to do... well, one does not quite know. In Charleston County, South Carolina, the school district had 30 of these individuals earning in excess of $100,000 as of 2013. In less than a decade, there were 103 additional administrators hitting that pay benchmark. This growth in high-pay administrative positions is a rising trend.

Of course, base salaries are but one aspect of compensation. Union bosses for years have fought to secure additional benefits such as generous pensions—and it has paid off. Consider this: between 2002 and 2019 (in other words, before the massive amounts of money injected into the system during and after COVID-19), the amount of taxpayer money spent on government schools increased by 20.7 percent after adjusting for inflation. But the majority of the funding—64.2 percent, to be precise—was spent on "growing benefits costs for both instructional and support staff, with instructional benefits accounting for roughly two-thirds of that growth."[7] Unsustainable spending suggests the need for cost cuts and drastic reforms to right the ship, yet teachers fight back. When the San Francisco Unified School District announced layoffs of up to 400 employees, the president of the local teachers' union claimed, "There is no financial reason to get rid of these vital educators, who provide essential instruction, services, and programs to students and their families." The district had a $125 million budget deficit.

Imagine for a moment that you were Elon Musk and you needed to determine who to fire at Twitter to reduce costs. How would you go about it? Would you reinterview all employees? Conduct peer evaluations to source input from the crowd? Among other potential data points, Twitter's new leadership looked at how many code commits employees had—in other words, who was most actively contributing directly to the product.[8] Who was innovating and creating new features? This trackable metric enabled Musk's team to initially identify the essential and productive employees who were directly connected to the product. Therefore, everyone else not committing code would have a harder time justifying their position and would have to go to greater lengths to make clear their value to the company's product.

Now imagine operating along these lines with government schools—measuring teacher performance based on a particular metric and making compensation and hiring decisions accordingly. This level of accountability is repulsive to those who have grown accustomed to their situation, as was famously depicted in *Office Space* when the HR team interviewing employees in order to determine who to fire struggled to understand what Tom did. After peppering him with questions in an effort to find *something* important or productive that he did, one of them exasperatingly blurted out to Tom: "What would you say... ya *do* here?"

Enter the National Education Association (NEA), which cares more about job security than quality educational services. At their convention in 2000, thousands of teachers supported a resolution saying "that performance pay schedules, such as merit pay or any other system of compensation based on an evaluation of an education employee's performance, are inappropriate."[9] Sometimes sunlight is the best disinfectant, and government schools could surely use a lot of it.

CIRCUMVENTING CURRICULUM RESTRICTIONS

"I'm ashamed that I'm White."

So said a seven-year-old girl to her mother in early 2021. "Is there something wrong with me?" she continued. "Why am I hated so much?"[1] This girl, a student at Liberty Elementary School in Franklin, Tennessee, was put in therapy by her mother, who explained that she is depressed, doesn't want to attend school anymore, and "has even had thoughts of killing herself." This mother was one of around 150 concerned parents who gathered to ask the Williamson County school superintendent questions about a variety of topics, including why critical race theory (CRT) was being taught to students. The superintendent declined to show up for his planned meeting.[2]

Across the country, parents have been appalled to see their children taught that they are part of an oppressive system simply because of their skin color. This is the intentional byproduct of CRT, which argues that our society and its institutions are implicitly racist with White people long in power who render others powerless. Proponents of this philosophy advance their agenda through criticizing (hence the "critical" part of CRT) our society in order to modify it. In the words of Richard Delgado, one of the architects of CRT, this agenda involves attacking the very foundations upon which America was built, including the idea of equality under the law as well as "legal reasoning, Enlightenment rationalism, and neutral principles of constitutional law."[3]

Once relegated to select college campuses and their echo chambers of postmodern neo-Marxism, the ideas have been taught to teachers and introduced through curricula and, thus, have found their way into K-12 schools across the country. Initially just the domain of history classes—where students were taught that the American colonists declared independence from Great Britain "to protect the institution of slavery" and that "this nation was founded not as a democracy but as a slavocracy"[4]—the anti-White campaign content has been snuck into all kinds of subjects, from civics and English literature to science and even math.[5]

Despite countless children being taught about their "White privilege" and being exposed to left-wing CRT ideology, the initial response by the school establishment was to deny it was even happening. "Let's be clear," said Randi Weingarten, head of the American Federation of Teachers, "critical race theory is *not* taught in elementary schools or high schools."[6] "Critical Race Theory is not taught in elementary school," claimed Congresswoman Alexandria Ocasio-Cortez.[7] MSNBC host Joy Reid argued that "law school is really the only place [CRT] is taught."[8] But these denials didn't hold much sway against a tsunami of parental concern and evidence of teachers pushing White guilt onto their students. So elected officials across the country responded by beginning to ban CRT in the classroom.[9]

That didn't sit well with the teachers' unions. The National Education Association passed a resolution in response saying they "oppose attempts to ban critical race theory and/or The 1619 Project," and they would promote curriculum that "critiques empire, white supremacy, anti-Blackness, anti-Indigeneity, racism, patriarchy, cisheteropatriarchy, capitalism, ableism, anthropocentrism, and other forms of power and oppression at the intersections of our society."[10] And with full disregard of the laws being passed restricting their ability to convey this content in the classroom, many teachers are continuing as they please.

Take Iowa, for example. The governor there signed a law that banned schools from teaching children "the idea that one race or sex is inherently superior to another race or sex, that the United States of America and the state of Iowa are fundamentally or systemically racist or sexist."[11] Critical race theory was not mentioned by name—instead, legislators tried to focus on the concepts being promoted in order to signal to government teachers that they should avoid these ideas in the classroom. But that hasn't stopped activist teachers from plowing forward. Anthony Ferguson, the executive director for "equity, inclusion, and diversity" at West Des Moines Community Schools said his teachers get around the ban by relabeling CRT. "I think we can do a lot of this work without the label and just do the work, right?" he said. "I don't have to call it critical race theory to know what we're doing."[12] Or take Ryan Williamson, the "equity and inclusion coordinator" at Urbandale Community School District, who said that the state's ban "hasn't affected us at all. Have we had to shift our language? Absolutely." He added, "It hasn't stopped us from talking about privilege."[13]

Iowa is certainly not alone; many other states have seen similar circumventions around their curriculum restrictions. When Idaho lawmakers cracked down on the promotion of social-emotional learning in the classroom—a seemingly innocuous focus on self-control and character development that has morphed into things like "justice-oriented civic engagement" for children[14]—school administrators ignored them. "Social-emotional learning, we can't say that here anymore," admitted Cindy Dion, an instructional coach at the Nampa school district in northern Idaho. Now, it's relabeled as mental health. "It's just our mental health curriculum. We're just learning how to worm around all those weird [restrictions] that are out there."[15] The chief academic officer for Caldwell School District, Melissa Langan, agreed with this strategic disregard for any meaningful curriculum restrictions. "I just went to a superintendent's meeting last week and the district was intending to switch out social-emotional learning to 'behavior adaptations,'" she said. "Changed the label, same stuff. And I thought, it's kind of a bummer they have to do that, but at the time I thought it was kind of brilliant. Because [concerned parents] don't care about [behavior adaptations] even though it's the same as [social-emotional learning]. But it's the label. So, I thought it was brilliant on their part."[16] Langan agreed that the same approach should be taken with CRT.

Across the country, these curriculum restrictions effectively accomplished nothing because as many school administrators conceded, "These teachers can close the door and do whatever they want."[17] And as bad as this all is, consider what is worse: There is far more that teachers are pushing onto students and doing in the classroom than parents and elected officials know; what has bubbled up to the surface is likely only the tip of the iceberg. What else is happening without the knowledge and consent of parents and the taxpayers who fund these institutions?

POLITICS > EDUCATION

We all know that government officials and those in the corporate media typically rank near the bottom when people are asked which professions they trust. But teachers are now sinking to the bottom as well. A Gallup poll conducted in January 2022 found that Americans rated the "honest and ethical standards" of teachers with a D grade—only 64 percent of adults indicated that they believe grade-school teachers are worthy of trust.[1] This score was an all-time low.

A few months after that poll, another one revealed that only 28 percent of Americans have high confidence in government schools[2]—the second-lowest score since Gallup started asking this question regularly in 1973.[3] Perhaps another way to slice the data is to understand how the teaching profession is itself perceived. Put more simply: do parents encourage their kids to become teachers, and do students aspire to enter the profession? While 75 percent of parents wanted a child of theirs to become a government school teacher in 1969, when this polling question was first recorded, since that time the response has averaged around

60 percent, and that figure has now plummeted to only 37 percent.

Perhaps it's obvious why this should matter. If trust in government schools and their teachers continues to dwindle, then families with sufficient resources will withdraw their children in search of superior educational opportunities. (And more states will pass policies like Education Savings Accounts, unlocking taxpayer dollars so they follow the child rather than remaining trapped in a degraded institution fewer students attend.) And in light of what has been deemed a "catastrophic teacher shortage,"[4] even fewer people will sign up for the profession, causing supply constraints that increase class size, decrease student and parental satisfaction, and continue the vicious cycle until the system irreparably breaks down—causing a lot of harm for students along the way.

As is common in many industries, the teaching profession has self-organized into an association to try and tackle these problems head on. The National Education Association (NEA)—commonly known as a teachers' union—describes itself as "the nation's largest professional employee organization" and "is committed to advancing the cause of public education."[5] With a membership exceeding three million people, the organization states, "Our vision is a great public school for every student." But does this aspirational statement reflect the reality of how this politically powerful group actually operates?

In 2019, over 6,000 NEA members gathered in Houston, Texas, for the organization's "Representative Assembly"—a gathering of teachers serving as delegates to represent the broader group. "It was amazing to see the dedication of teachers... and how much each of us care about our students," said one attendee.[6] "I was able to watch firsthand how we as educators hold the power to make changes in our classrooms, state, nation and beyond," remarked another.[7] As part of their official business, these teachers and thousands more considered a variety of resolutions, including one that read:

> The National Education Association will re-dedicate itself to the pursuit of increased student learning in every public school in America by putting a renewed emphasis on quality education. *NEA will make student learning the priority of the Association.* NEA will not waiver in its commitment to student learning by adopting the following lens through which we will assess every NEA program and initiative: How does the proposed action promote the development of students as lifelong reflective learners?[8]

The proposal failed.

Just ponder the situation for a moment. Thousands of teachers, gathered to represent millions more, were asked to publicly commit to doing the very thing that all of us think that their profession exists to do: make student learning and quality education a priority. And they shrugged. Meanwhile, delegates favorably approved resolutions endorsing "the fundamental right to abortion under *Roe v. Wade*," supporting reparations for slave descendants, and lauding the Black Lives Matter movement as well as the teaching of "White Fragility" in NEA professional development efforts.[9]

If this sounds like teachers are more focused on radical left-wing politics than quality education, it might sound that way because it is true. Consider another metric that indicates teachers are more focused on wielding political power than prioritizing pedagogy. Members of the nation's two largest teachers' unions funnel nearly all their political donations to Democrats. In the 2022 election cycle, 99.99 percent of campaign contributions from the American Federation of Teachers went to Democrats,[10] and 98.93 percent of campaign contributions from the NEA went to Democrats.[11]

Sometimes the truth comes straight from the horse's mouth. When he retired from his position as general counsel of the National Education Association,

Bob Chanin stood before the assembled teachers at one of their conventions in 2009 to speak frankly, saying that the NEA was effective "because we have power."[12] And that power was the dues they collected—the hundreds of millions of dollars raised and then funneled to Democrats. Chanin decried the "conservative and right-wing bastards picking on NEA and its affiliates" because they "are the nation's leading advocates for... the type of liberal social and economic agenda that these groups find unacceptable."[13] And while student success might happen for some students, Chanin made clear that if helping students came at the expense of union power, it was "too high a price to pay."[14]

We all know good teachers dedicated to helping students excel, but the system itself is horribly corrupt and infiltrated with left-wing political activists more interested in professional self-preservation than student learning.

INFORMATION OVER INQUIRY

Ben Orlin is a high school math teacher in Oakland, California. When he addressed the assembled students in his first-ever trigonometry class, he asked them what the sine of $\pi/2$ is. Their unified answer, "One!" indicated that they had already covered the material. "We learned that last year," they told their teacher.

Like any new teacher, Orlin zipped ahead through the material, but came to realize that the students didn't know what "sine" actually meant—they had merely memorized the answer to the question. "To them," Orlin writes, "math wasn't a process of logical discovery and thoughtful exploration. It was a call-and-response game. Trigonometry was just a collection of non-rhyming lyrics to the lamest sing-along ever."[1]

For well over a century, government schools have been producing generations of human automatons—robotically programmed people educated for the purpose of producing predictable outputs. Government schools—designed for a factory-style economy in which individuals had a specific, repeatable task to be replicated consistently, requiring them to follow orders and stay in their lane—have not meaningfully innovated beyond this original design. The mindset that permeates this system is one of "information upload" where "students are to be filled with all the appropriate data and applications to function as cogs in the machinery of factories and offices, or in the parlance of today, as walking hard drives."[2] But as Orlin notes, this information-heavy approach to education is not ideal:

> Some things are worth memorizing—addresses, PINs, your parents' birthdays. The sine of $\pi/2$ is not among them. It's a fact that matters only insofar as it connects to other ideas. To learn it in isolation is like learning the sentence "Hamlet kills Claudius" without the faintest idea of who either gentleman is—or, for that matter, of what "kill" means. Memorization is a frontage road: It runs parallel to the best parts of learning, never intersecting. It's a detour around all the action, a way of knowing without learning, of answering without understanding.[3]

Government schools prioritize regurgitation of information over actual knowledge comprehension and application. This rote memorization and forced learning gives the appearance of knowledge mastery while masking the reality of inadequate understanding. It destroys curiosity and exploration, dumbing down the education process into repeatable tidbits of information to be crammed into one's mind for an upcoming test. As one college professor observed, these dysfunctional effects create problems for students as they mature.

> After years of cramming, memorizing, regurgitating, and forgetting, many students enter college with little intellectual curiosity, much less a sense of academic excitement. Too often, the students just want to be told what they need to learn to pass the test or what they need to write to get a good grade on a paper. Because so much of their schooling has been based on this dysfunctional model, they have forgotten how to be the self-directed and genuine learners that they were when they first entered school.[4]

It is no wonder that a system designed to inculcate information instead of cultivate inquiry and exploration has degraded into mediocrity. The authoritarian model of government schools in which information is imparted from the teacher and textbook into the child's mind does not facilitate the cognitive development required to become a curious, critical thinker—someone who learns *how*, instead of only learning *what*. This model encourages students to be passive participants in the process, simply receiving and regurgitating knowledge shared by the teacher through didactic teaching methods.

Imagine you want to become a surfer. No sane person would think that this goal can be achieved by listening to lectures and reading from a book. Breaking down the various skills into teachable tidbits won't get the student very far; learning how to wax your board well, balance on it, and catch a wave at the right moment isn't something that can be verbally shown. It has to be demonstrated and experienced. The same applies to mastering cognitive skills—learning *how* to think. If you don't experience the need to use them in an educational setting, they won't develop.

Unfortunately, government schools have little to no incentive to change their learning model. Entire industries of teachers' unions and other special interests have arisen to defend the status quo and protect their turf from competition. Electing different school board members has historically not produced significant change to the school system itself, and enterprising teachers can only do so much to modify their instruction while still staying compliant with state standards imposed upon them. For the foreseeable future, then, government schools will continue to prioritize information over inquiry, producing generations of cognitively deficient adults who have been trained to remember and regurgitate factoids. Mediocrity indeed.

STUDENTS TREATED AS POLITICAL PAWNS

While we hope that nothing like COVID-19—and the government policies enforced in its wake—happens ever again, it would be naive to assume that what we witnessed was completely anomalous. While future circumstances will no doubt be different, we can better prepare for future challenges by learning from past problems. As the saying goes, "Those who don't learn from the past are condemned to repeat it."

What happened with schools during the pandemic offers many observations to learn from—among them, how students were treated as political pawns by those entrusted to support them. This should not be surprising, of course; government schools are inherently political because they are created, funded, and overseen by political entities. But parents generally enroll their children to receive a quality education, not to be ignored or used as props for the political goals of those who control these institutions.

For example, one of the fiercest debates in 2020 and 2021 involved the question of when to reopen the government schools that had nearly all been shuttered by dictatorial decree. What was initially a decision made by political leaders, often at the urging of public health officials, had become a completely political question void of scientific guidance. Research indicates that "School districts in locations with stronger teachers' unions [were] less likely to reopen in person" and "School closures [were] uncorrelated with the actual incidence of the virus."[1] Additional research found that "mass partisanship and vested interests best explain the degree to which schools reopened. Republican districts were far more likely to reopen in person, while districts with stronger unions relied more on remote learning."[2] And just as monopolies can often get away with bad decisions until they are threatened by competition, "public schools were sensitive to the threat of student exit. Districts located in counties with more Catholic schools were somewhat more likely to reopen in person."[3] In other words, it wasn't actually about science—it was about the political views and personal preferences of teachers and school administrators.

The competitive outcomes in counties with more Catholic schools was probably because those government school leaders understood that families with more relatively low-cost exit options could vote with their feet. The main difference is one of incentives. While private schools consistently fought to remain open, many teachers' unions fought to keep government schools closed for over a year despite substantial evidence[4] suggesting that schools could reopen safely. Only one of these sectors gets your money regardless of whether they open their doors for business.

And these people were political players, not passive observers of the school closure decisions being made. Emails uncovered by a Freedom of Information Act request revealed that, on at least two occasions, language suggested by the American Federation of Teachers (one of the major teachers' unions) was included nearly verbatim in the CDC's guidance on safely reopening schools.[5] "Thank you again for Friday's rich discussion about forthcoming CDC guidance and for your openness to the suggestions made by our president, Randi Weingarten, and the AFT," one of their directors wrote in an email—which described the union as the CDC's "thought partner." The NEA was also involved in discussions with White House personnel and the CDC, and a senior official at the US Department of Health and Human Services cautioned colleagues: "We need to think about [school reopenings] in the broader context of teacher contract negotiations."[6] The suggestions and interference from these highly political organizations were not based on science—they were maneuvers to put the unions in a better position to keep government schools closed and bargain for more resources and benefits from taxpayers.

Take United Teachers Los Angeles, for example. This union's membership includes more than 35,000 teachers in the country's second-largest school district. As pressure mounted to reopen schools, the group pushed back and demanded things like "an immediate moratorium on new charter schools... the passage of Medicare for All, new state-level wealth taxes in California, and a federal bailout of the [school district]—which is struggling to meet pension obligations for retired teachers and staff."[7] Other unions across the country joined together to demand "a national ban on evictions, a moratorium on charter schools, an end to voucher programs, and the abolition of standardized testing. They also want a 'massive infusion of federal money'... paid for by, of course, 'taxing billionaires and Wall Street.'"[8] Student safety and science-based health guidelines were secondary to the broader political goals by these left-leaning activists.

Again, the wrong reaction to all of this is to write it off as an unfortunate but unique set of conditions that are unlikely to reoccur in the future. What is evident from the experience is students are too often treated as political pawns and their concerns ignored when they do not align with or benefit the political views and personal preferences of the massive industry that has emerged to school them. While we cannot predict the type of future challenges that might develop, it seems reasonable to suggest that the education outcomes and well-being of students may once again take a backseat to the political agendas of those who wield influence in government schools.

TEACHER KNOWS BEST?

"This will be horrifying for me to read to you," Kandra Evans told school board members in Clark County, Nevada, at a May 2022 meeting. Her voice quivered, revealing the deep emotion she was feeling about what her fifteen-year-old daughter had been assigned by her school teacher. "But that will give you perspective on how she must have felt when her teacher required her to memorize this and to act it out in front of her entire class."[1]

Evans proceeded to read several sentences of dialogue between two people, with one speaking crudely about male genitalia. The school board chairwoman interrupted, "Forgive me, we're not using profanity." Evans appeared visibly confused by the commotion that had erupted after she read what her young daughter was required to memorize and repeat. "If you don't want me to read it to you, what was it like for my 15-year-old daughter to have to memorize pornographic material and memorize it?" she asked.[2]

Michelle Brown had a similar experience when speaking at a school board meeting in Cherokee County, Georgia. "Here's an excerpt," she began, "and I'm going to really try to be careful so I don't get kicked out."[3] Brown began reading an excerpt of a book she objected to that was available to school students, which described intercourse in explicit detail between two characters.

"Excuse me, we have children at home," one school board member interjected, pointing out that the meeting was being live-streamed and calling the passage "inappropriate."[4]

"Don't you find the irony in that?" Brown responded. "You're exactly saying exactly what I'm telling you! You're giving it to our children! I would never give this to my children!"[5]

Passionate parents across the country have been speaking up out of concern for what is being taught in schools, and rather than being received by a welcome audience of public servants appreciative for their engagement and input, they are often met with hostility and derision. In New Jersey, the local teachers' union was so fed up with this trend that they produced a video ad calling such parents "extremists," adding, "People who only want to fight to score political points should take that somewhere else."[6] It is especially ironic that a political organization like a teachers' union derisively dismisses parental concerns as "political points" to be "scored," as if these parents are playing some kind of game.

At the root of this parental pushback seems to be the idea that parents are inferior stakeholders when it comes to the education and intellectual development of their own children. This teacher-knows-best mentality has been expressed by many, such as former Virginia Governor McAuliffe who publicly stated, "I don't think parents should be telling schools what they should teach." And when Senator Tim Scott said, "We are putting parents back in charge of their kids' education," Representative Eric Swalwell replied:

> Please tell me what I'm missing here. What are we doing next? Putting patients in charge of their own surgeries? Clients in charge of their own trials? When did we stop trusting experts. This is so stupid.[7]

Not to be outdone by these individual politicians, the National Education Association weighed in to double down: "Educators love their students," the large teachers' union said, "and know *better than anyone* what they need to learn and to thrive."[8] Perhaps the best reply was this snarky one from former US Secretary of Education Betsy DeVos: "You misspelled parents."[9]

One might reasonably assume that if school teachers knew—better than anyone—what children need to learn, then America's schools would not be drowning under the rising tide of mediocrity with consistently low test scores and educational outcomes for students. If the millions of teachers, allegedly represented by the unions, indeed know what is best, why haven't we seen them achieve anything close to it? The question answers itself.

What is especially concerning, though, is the apparent entitlement mentality this situation reveals—a collectivist attitude where school administrators and teachers feel like these students belong to them. For example, President Joe Biden said, speaking to a group of teachers, "They're all our children... They're not somebody else's [each parents'] children. They're like yours when they're in the classroom."[10] This was previously echoed by Melissa Harris-Perry, an MSNBC commentator and professor of political science:

> We have never invested as much in public education as we should have because we've always had a private notion of children, [that] your kid is yours and totally your responsibility. We haven't had a very collective notion of these are *our* children.
>
> So part of it is we have to break through our kind of private idea that kids belong to their parents,

or kids belong to their families, and recognize that kids belong to *whole communities*.[11]

It is this domineering and dismissive attitude that pervades many school campuses and school boards, creating an animus that pits parents against the public servants who, in theory, serve them. To these people, parental rights are an inconvenience and roadblock; parents are perceived to be a nuisance rather than a partner or customer.

SEXUAL ABUSE, AGAIN AND AGAIN

Cori Beard seemingly had soccer in her DNA. At Vernon Hills High School in Chicago, Illinois, she was a star player and a member of the All-Sectional, All-Area, and All-Conference teams. In her senior year, she was captain of the team. Beard's father was a coach for forty years and had been inducted into the High School Soccer Coaches Association Hall of Fame. "To me there's no better job than being a soccer coach," he once told reporters.[1]

Beard graduated from high school in 2006, played soccer in college, and then was hired as an assistant soccer coach for the boys and girls soccer teams at her former high school. She had the privilege of coaching alongside her father, surely a great experience for the two of them—until it became a disaster.

While working alongside her father, Beard began a sexual relationship with multiple boys she had coached. She was in her mid-to-late twenties, and the boys were in their early teens.[2] Prosecutors charged Beard with multiple counts of sexual assault, most of which were ultimately dropped in exchange for a plea deal in which she admitted guilt and was sentenced to six years in prison, followed by two years of probation, community service, and potential treatment programs.[3]

This story is not an outlier; there are countless examples of teachers and others in positions of trust in schools creating unlawful sexual relationships with minors.[4] In 2022, for example, there was nearly one child sex crime a day in K-12 schools in the United States; one analysis in October of that year found that 269 educators had been arrested for such crimes—including "four principals, two assistant principals, 226 teachers, 20 teacher's aides. and 17 substitute teachers."[5]

Here is a question: where is the outrage? By comparison, consider what happened when there was a widespread investigation and exposure of sex abuse in the Catholic Church in the early 2000s. In 2002, *The Boston Globe* published a Pulitzer Prize-winning series of stories covering sexual abuse cases involving Catholic priests. The team of journalists—most of them Catholic and residents of the largest Catholic city in America—ended up producing 800 articles on the scandal. Within two years, "150 priests in Boston stood accused of sexual abuse, more than 500 victims had filed abuse claims, and church-goers' donations to the archdiocese had slumped by 50%."[6] One study published shortly after *The Boston Globe*'s reporting found that for the past half a century, "4,392 Catholic priests and deacons in active ministry... [were] plausibly (neither withdrawn nor disproven) accused of under-age sexual abuse by 10,667 individuals."[7] Public reaction was swift, media coverage was substantial, and the Church was pressured into a number of apologies, investigations, and reforms.

Now compare the sexual abuse in Catholic Churches to government schools. A study published by the US Department of Education in 2004—just two years after *The Boston Globe*'s stories began—found that the best available data points to "nearly 9.6 percent of students [being] targets of educator sexual misconduct sometime during their school career."[8] Based on that research, the scale of sexual abuse in government schools "is nearly 100 times greater than that of the Catholic Church."[9] How many more teachers have to get arrested before this trend turns into a scandal as it did for the Catholic Church? How many more children need to be sexually abused by the adults they're expected to trust before some serious reforms take place? And how many hundreds of millions of dollars will taxpayers be required to shell out in settlements and court-mandated awards to victims before real change happens?

Of course, it's not just adults who are the problem here. The Associated Press spent a year investigating sexual abuse by students themselves, using data for five years from 2011 to 2015. They identified roughly 17,000 cases during that period, creating the "most complete tally yet of sexual assaults among the nation's 50 million K-12 students."[10] But despite the breadth of evidence, their research did not "fully capture the problem because such attacks are greatly under-reported, some states don't track them, and those that do vary widely in how they classify and catalog sexual violence."[11] The data this team of journalists uncovered found that "For every adult-on-child sexual attack reported on school property, there were seven assaults by students."[12] Think about this: if sexual abuse by teachers is nearly one hundred times greater than it was in the Catholic Church, and if sexual abuse by students is seven times greater than *that*, we're dealing with a staggering problem that dwarfs the church scandal and yet receives extraordinarily little media attention. And even worse, despite having long been put on notice by the US Supreme Court, schools "frequently were unwilling or ill-equipped to address the problem."[13] Even worse, some actively oppose measures designed to help; in Rhode Island, for example, the two teachers' unions fought a bill that would have made it a crime for a school employee to have sex with a student under age eighteen.[14]

This problem is far, far worse than mere mediocrity. Parents expect their children to be kept safe and treated with respect. Schools exist, in theory, to educate and support a child—not to make them vulnerable to abuse from adults or peers. Caring parents need to seriously reevaluate whether such an environment is best for their children and whether the trade-offs are worth it.

MO' BUREAUCRACY, MO' MEDIOCRITY

Jeremy Tate is passionate about education. As a teacher, a college counselor, and later a director of an SAT preparatory company, he was "shocked to discover how much the test had changed" since he had taken it as a high school senior—and was alarmed at how the test "championed the views of the political left."[1] So he founded Classic Learning Test, an alternative to the SAT and ACT, that helps measure the values parents actually want to instill in their children, grounded in the liberal arts tradition.

Tate's experience is similar to countless others who are prompted to take action once they realize how bad a particular problem is. But without that exposure—without realizing the significance of the problem—oftentimes solutions aren't realized. (That's also the purpose of this book, by the way—to shock you into seeing just how bad the status quo is and the need for education solutions for your children and everyone else's.) When problems are well understood, then we can begin talking about how to fix them.

Tate was in the same ignorance trap on a related issue: the benefits and purpose of the US Department of Education. "The first time I heard somebody say [it] should not exist," he wrote, "I thought they were nuts." It's easy to dismiss a problem when everyone around you agrees among themselves that it isn't actually a problem. "Then they asked me to list just one academic metric that has improved since its inception in 1980. I couldn't. Nobody can."[2]

Originally proposed in the 1860s by leaders of what is now the National Education Association teachers' union, the federal office was in the past housed under various cabinet-level departments until President Jimmy Carter signed a law in 1979, elevating it to its own cabinet status and giving it an annual budget of over $12 billion (over $50 billion in today's dollars).[3] This change, made late in Carter's first term, was a political favor to the NEA (who had been lobbying for a cabinet-level department for years[4]) in an effort to shore up their support for his reelection in light of his sinking poll numbers.[5] He was the first presidential candidate the teachers' union had endorsed after his running mate had promised them at their 1976 annual meeting that a Carter administration would form an education department. As the NEA's own executive director once boasted, "There'd be no department without the NEA."[6] Not all Democrats were in lockstep at the time; more than one-third of House Democrats voted against the bill.[7] One of them said, "The idea of an Education Department is really a bad one. But it's NEA's top priority. There are school teachers in every congressional district and most of us simply don't need the aggravation of taking them on."[8] Here's what President Carter stated after creating the standalone department—

> ...the Federal Government has for too long failed to play its own supporting role in education as effectively as it could. Instead of assisting school officials at the local level, it has too often added to their burden. Instead of setting a strong administrative model, the Federal structure has contributed to bureaucratic buck passing. Instead of simulating needed debate of educational issues, the Federal Government has confused its role of junior partner in American education with that of silent partner.[9]

To address the existing "bureaucratic buck passing," a new bureaucracy was created. Decades later, the US Department of Education now has 4,400 employees and an annual budget of $68 billion.[10] And Tate was right—education outcomes have not improved in the past several decades; the tide of mediocrity has only risen further. Multiple trillions of dollars have been spent on this federal department alone—and for what? More mediocrity, more "bureaucratic buck passing," and stagnant, low education outcomes—especially for children from poor, rural, or immigrant families.

One former US secretary of education agrees. "I think the department should not exist," Betsy DeVos once said. "The federal department of education does not add any value to kids' education... It is not involved in education in a good and positive and constructive way."[11] As a government agency, it has been weaponized for political purposes—certainly neither positively nor constructively. After DeVos's departure, the department clashed with Florida Governor Ron DeSantis, who in August 2021 signed an executive order to protect a parent's right to determine whether their child would wear a mask at school. DeSantis's administration punished school districts that ignored his executive order by withholding the salaries of school board members in those districts. In response, Miguel Cardona—the succeeding secretary after DeVos—said that the Department of Education would "do everything in our power to provide a safe environment for our students and staff to thrive," and added that any penalties imposed by DeSantis's team would be replaced by federal relief funds.[12]

Hiring thousands of bureaucrats and spending trillions of taxpayer dollars has not improved education outcomes. It has siphoned money away from families that they could better put to use to support their children, and it has interfered with parental rights and family autonomy in education. It's time to put this federal department out to pasture.

SOPHISTICATED SCHOOL SEGREGATION

In theory, government schools exist to be society's great equalizer—to help children of diverse backgrounds, especially those in less fortunate circumstances, gain the skills necessary to achieve the American Dream. In practice, government schools exacerbate the inequities they were meant to cure.

Nearly two centuries ago, Horace Mann set out on a campaign to import the Prussian model of education and create a "common school" movement that homogenized families from diverse socioeconomic backgrounds into one "American" identity—a large-scale, social engineering effort as much as it was a pedagogical one. Mann believed that education "is the great equalizer of the conditions of men, the balance-wheel of the social machinery."[1] Level the playing field, and give everyone a fair shot—that was (again, at least in theory) the idea.

Mann's movement spilled over into the constitutional debates happening as more states were being added to the union. Today, every state has a provision in its constitution requiring the legislature to provide for public (government) schooling. Arkansas requires a "suitable and efficient system of free public schools" in order to "secure to the people the advantages and opportunities of education."[2] Wyoming requires "a complete and uniform system of public instruction."[3] And in New York, "a system of free common schools" is constitutionally obligated, "wherein all the children of this state may be educated."[4] But the high-minded language in many states was not universal; Alabama, for example, added a provision that "no child of either race shall be permitted to attend a school of the other race."[5] Neighborhood schools in southern states were captured by White residents to the exclusion of Black children in the area; other states acted similarly with respect to Hispanic or Asian students, as in California where the law said, "Negroes, Mongolians and Indians shall not be allowed into public schools."[6]

This school segregation was stopped in 1954 by the landmark *Brown v. Board* of Education opinion issued by the US Supreme Court. But a more sophisticated kind of school segregation persists—one that discriminates not on how a child looks but rather where the child happens to live. Decades after the *Brown* ruling, many government schools in America remain out of reach to low-income families whose finances don't allow them to live within the "attendance zones" drawn around the best schools. A child's educational fate is too often determined by an arbitrary line on a map. "In many American cities, this means that living on one side of the street or the other will determine whether you leave eighth grade on a track for future success or barely able to read."[7]

A geographical segregation of students allows for discrimination by financial ability—so-called free government schools are not all created equal, so the schools in wealthier areas of town attract more resources, better teachers, and a superior learning environment. And yes, government schools operate in lower-income areas to serve the students there, but the inverse is true here: these schools typically have fewer resources, worse teachers, and an inferior learning environment. Jackie Nowicki, the director of K-12 education at the Government Accountability Office, points out that "large portions of minority children [are] not only attending essentially segregated schools, but schools that have less resources available to them."[8] Her team researched this modern school segregation and found that "more than a third of students (about 18.5 million of them) attended a predominantly same-race/ethnicity school during the 2020-21 school year."[9]

While *Brown v. Board of Education* prohibited the "letter of the law" segregation, the "spirit of the law" persists through policies and laws that exclude students from admission based on where they live—an indirect indicator of their socioeconomic status and potential proxy, in part, for their ethnicity. "There are historical reasons why neighborhoods look the way they look," Nowicki explains. "And some portion of that is because of the way our country chose to encourage or limit where people could live."[10]

The geographic (and indirectly racial) segregation of students is rather unique to schools. In what other industry are people excluded from participation because of where they live? Are you asked about your ZIP code when entering the grocery store or taking your children to a park in another town? If you want to use the landfill one county over, or golf on a government-owned course in another state, are you denied entry because of the location of where you reside? Imagine being on vacation and taking your children to the local public library only to be barred entry because you don't live within their "neighborhood zone." We would find it preposterous—abjectly stupid, in fact—to deny people access to these taxpayer-funded resources on the basis of where they live. Why, then, do we tolerate this system when it comes to education?

CONFORMITY OVER CURIOSITY

On June 25, 2010, eighteen-year-old Erica Goldson stood at a podium in front of her peers and their parents. Behind her sat her school's administrators and teachers. As school valedictorian, Erica now had the opportunity to speak to her graduating class.

To say that Erica's words were unexpected would be a tremendous understatement. The speech was akin to dropping a grenade into a foxhole filled with both wounded warriors and war generals. It rebuked the very institution in which she excelled and condemned the life work of the salaried school staff who supported her. But while many took offense, others received inspiration from the accurate and honest assessment of the problems Erica and her peers had navigated.

"I cannot say that I am any more intelligent than my peers," Erica said. "I can attest that I am only the best at doing what I am told and working the system." She continued:

> Yet, here I stand, and I am supposed to be proud that I have completed this period of indoctrination. I will leave in the fall to go on to the next

phase expected of me, in order to receive a paper document that certifies that I am capable of work. But I contest that I am a human being, a thinker, an adventurer—not a worker. A worker is someone who is trapped within repetition—a slave of the system set up before him. But now, I have successfully shown that I was the best slave. I did what I was told to the extreme.[1]

Ouch.

If the modern education system is a conveyor belt of manufactured learning, then Erica was the Grade A product—the very best commodity the system had produced. She was superior to the rest, jumping through every hoop and following the system's guidelines to the letter. But at what cost? Erica explains:

> While others sat in class and doodled to later become great artists, I sat in class to take notes and become a great test-taker.

> While others would come to class without their homework done because they were reading about an interest of theirs, I never missed an assignment.

> While others were creating music and writing lyrics, I decided to do extra credit, even though I never needed it.

So, I wonder, why did I even want this position? Sure, I earned it, but what will come of it? When I leave educational institutionalism, will I be successful or forever lost? I have no clue about what I want to do with my life; I have no interests because I saw every subject of study as work, and I excelled at every subject just for the purpose of excelling, not learning. And quite frankly, now I'm scared.[2]

If a model student like Erica is terrified of her future, and ill-equipped to face it, then what is the point of the system at all? The quality of output compels us to question the process used to create it. What this speech lays bare is the problem where schools prioritize conformity over curiosity—the conveyor belt over a child's unique path. The standardization of schooling is not without merit; it seems quite a difficult task to build a centralized education model that can accommodate the diverse backgrounds, interests, and curiosities of countless children and support them in pursuing these varying paths. How could a teacher of thirty children realistically oversee such a system, let alone a superintendent over thousands? In the name of organizational efficiency, and since it is not feasible for schools to adapt to such diverse students, the centralized model must instead make students adapt to *it*.

Research shows that curious children have better education outcomes, and yet today's government schools are not structured to cultivate curiosity; all too often, it is suppressed—as in the case of one ninth grader who raised her hand to ask a question about art. Before she finished her question, the teacher interrupted, "Zoe, no questions now, please; it's time for learning."[3]

In 2007, researchers observed young children to log how many questions they were asking. Those between fourteen months and five years of age asked an average of 107 questions an hour; one child "was asking three questions a minute at his peak."[4] But additional research shows that "questioning drops like a stone once children start school"; the youngest children in school asked between two to five questions in a two-hour class period. Worse than that, "There were two-hour stretches in fifth grade where 10- and 11-year-olds failed to ask their teacher a single question."[5] Students learn to be quiet and do what they're told—to conform instead of explore their curiosity.

Albert Einstein once wrote that it is "nothing short of a miracle that the modern methods of instruction have not yet entirely strangled the holy curiosity of inquiry; for this delicate little plant, aside from stimulation, stands mainly in need of freedom; without this it goes to wreck and ruin without fail. It is a very grave mistake to think that the enjoyment of seeing and searching can be promoted by means of coercion and a sense of duty." That, in a nutshell, is how government schools are failing millions of children.

TEACHING TO THE TEST

"The state tests being used to evaluate student progress—and, in turn, the effectiveness of teachers—virtually ensure mediocrity."[1]

That's the opinion of Kelly Gallagher, a teacher at Magnolia High School in Anaheim, California. At first blush, one might dismiss his objection to evaluation as part of the longstanding opposition shared by teachers' unions to measuring performance of teachers and conditioning their employment based on their results. After all, teachers have protested in the street to send "a clear message to our elected leaders... that education is about learning, not testing."[2] We know that what is measured improves—and so measuring the education outcomes of students is obviously essential, even if simply from a taxpayer investment standpoint.

But Gallagher's connection between testing and mediocrity reveals something more than this professional resistance to accountability. After all, he signed up to teach in order to help his students develop critical thinking skills. "I want my students to grow up to be problem-solvers, not test-takers. I want them to be innovators, not automatons," he wrote.[3] In concept, evaluation is important—but the devil is in the details (and in the incentives).

If teachers are evaluated based on the scores their students obtain on standardized tests, then those teachers are incentivized to ensure students excel—not in education generally, but in the standardized test specifically. "Teaching to the test" is a well-known problem in government schools that has been exacerbated into an education epidemic, especially as a result of the federal No Child Left Behind law that was implemented in 2002. This law, designed (in theory) to increase accountability, "virtually transformed the concept of education, turning teaching and learning into a mere exercise in prepping students to test well."[4] In hopes of looking good, teachers abandon the aspirational reasons, like Gallagher's, for which they signed up to teach in the first place—and they begin spending an inordinate amount of classroom time preparing their students for the tests.

The incentive also produces incentives of its own. Enterprising teachers and school administrators, hoping to look good, promise their students parties and prizes for good performance. Teachers at Ocean Springs Middle School in Mississippi put on a carnival for 400 eighth graders after doing well on their tests—a "reward to the eighth-graders and an incentive to the seventh-graders about to take the test,"[5] in the words of the PTA president. Or in Utah, after word got out that teachers were giving out candy and treats for certain test scores, the state legislature stepped in and passed a bill banning the practice, saying that teachers could not "reward a student for taking an assessment."[6] Even worse, some teachers respond to this incentive by cheating. In Atlanta, Georgia, more than 150 teachers and administrators from dozens of different schools in the city were caught changing students' test answers. "We were told to get these scores by any means necessary," one of the teachers said, adding, "We were told our jobs were on the line."[7] Eighty-two of the teachers confessed outright to a practice that had been going on for decades.

The primary problem of "teaching to the test" is that it deprives students of cognitive development opportunities by steering them more toward rote memorization; teachers who focus on the bits of knowledge that students are most likely to encounter on an exam will not have the time or energy to drill deep into the context of a particular subject matter. A study from 2012 found that teachers who focused on high-stakes testing "didn't prompt students to understand solutions conceptually as frequently or present challenging problems as often."[8] For example, one study found that in a school district that relied heavily on this teach-to-the-test methodology, 83 percent of students correctly answered a multiple-choice item written as "87 - 24 ="— a simple math formula with four possible answers provided. But when the question was open-ended— "Subtract 24 from 87," with no answers provided— only 66 percent of students could provide the correct answer.[9]

Evaluation is important, and teachers—like any other professional—should be held accountable for their performance. Only in this way can we sift out the substandard educators and praise and prize those who excel and better help children achieve superior education outcomes. But the incentives matter, as does the nature of the testing itself; after all, "standardized tests are only useful for measuring standardized minds."[10]

THE YOUNGER, THE BETTER

John Licata is a school board member in Buffalo, New York, and the driving force behind making kindergarten mandatory in the city. He was concerned that many six-year-olds were entering government schools without "the kind of social skills helpful in a classroom setting."[1] Voluntary kindergarten meant, in his view, that many parents "often don't take attendance for kindergarten classes seriously."[2] (Is finger painting and song time to be taken "seriously"?) So he crusaded to force families into enrolling their five-year-olds in school. "It's not the child who is the problem," Licata said. "It's the fact that it's not compulsory."[3] And beyond mandatory kindergarten enrollment, school administrators in Buffalo hoped that the requirement would "heighten interest by parents in sending their children to prekindergarten programs when they are four." Licata and his peers wanted to "front-load education when children are young, curious, and engaged, and that means making sure children attend kindergarten."[4]

Compulsory schooling has crept into younger years, with nineteen states and the District of Columbia legally requiring that children attend kindergarten.[5] And the "front-loading" to push more children into prekindergarten was something Dale Farran thought would be a positive. Farran, a researcher who spent a decade studying over a thousand children who went to a government prekindergarten, observed results that ran counter to what she expected. By sixth grade, and compared to a control group of children who didn't get into the pre-K schools, the children who began schooling that early were doing worse all around—scoring more poorly on math, reading, and science. They were also "more likely to have both learning disorders and disciplinary problems—including serious ones that got them suspended."[6] Farran was shocked by the discovery. "It really has required a lot of soul-searching," she admitted, hoping to find "plausible reasons that may account for this."[7] In a typical pre-K environment, children have unstructured play time, art and creativity, music, and more. But in these government-run institutions where they were required to provide young children with over five hours of "instructional time" each day, the children were compelled to trace letters, fill out worksheets, and listen to lectures. "The kids also spent a lot of time simply schlepping from one activity to another, while being told to pipe down and don't touch."[8] Remember that these were four-year-olds.

First established by Friederich Wilhelm Froebel in Germany in 1837, kindergarten (literally "garden of children") was envisioned as a school for toddlers. Froebel likened children to little flowers: "They are varied and need care, but each is beautiful alone and glorious when seen in the community of peers."[9] A century and a half later, as kindergarten had become a worldwide phenomenon—with the enrollment of children in government schools at an even younger age—the German government commissioned a study in the 1970s to determine whether it would be helpful to teach academic skills to this younger cohort or maintain kindergarten as Froebel envisioned it: a place for play, stories, and singing. One hundred kindergarten classes were selected for the study—fifty using some academic training in their activities and the other fifty abstaining from it. The results are not unlike what Farran found:

> The graduates of academic kindergartens performed better on academic tests in first grade than the others, but the difference subsequently faded, and by fourth grade they were performing worse than the others on every measure in the study. Specifically, they scored more poorly

on tests of reading and arithmetic and were less well-adjusted socially and emotionally than the controls.[10]

Not everyone agrees, of course. W. Steven Barnett directs the National Institute for Early Education Research. He believes that kindergarten matters a great deal and, when asked about a proposal in Philadelphia to change kindergarten from a full day to a half day, pointed out, "Cutting that time in half would create problems down the road, compelling teachers to spend more time on remedial courses and causing some students to be left back."[11] Or take Senator Susan Rubio, sponsor of a bill in California to make kindergarten mandatory, who argued that "students that do not attend miss fundamental instruction putting them at a disadvantage in a classroom setting as they enter first grade."[12] But the very fact that kindergarten now involves "fundamental instruction" that, if not sufficiently understood, requires "remediation" (a term once used mainly to describe courses for unprepared college students who needed to brush up on basic high school knowledge), highlights the basic problem. Childhood curiosity and unstructured play time is being pushed aside inappropriately, and at ever younger ages, to make way for rigorous academic standards for four- and five-year-olds.

Once upon a time, kids were free to be kids. Today, they are students from the start, front-loaded with fundamental instruction that can't be missed, lest they be left behind.

PUMP AND DUMP

What role should memorization play in learning at school? "As a social studies teacher, I am forever tormented by this question,"[1] said Sarah Cooper, an eighth-grade US history teacher at a school in California. Teaching in a time-limited environment—with learning stopped by a bell—makes teachers like her repeatedly decide which information to superficially present and have children memorize and which information to teach with deep context and real-life comprehension. Cooper continued:

> Those of us who teach social studies and science, especially, with facts and information coming out of our ears, engage in endless compromises: what to dive into, what to gloss over, and what we hope someone, somewhere, tells our students someday because we certainly won't have time this year.[2]

For her part, she focuses on requiring the memorization of dates and facts that create "scaffolding, a framework on which to hang future knowledge."[3] For example, a student might be required to memorize key dates during the American Revolution in order to have some basic orientation around the timeline that would inform future learning by placing events in the right order. And while this makes sense, for many students it is the exception—memorization turns from scaffolding to the structure of learning itself, especially in classrooms where incentives push educators to "teach to the test" and optimize for memory recall to perform well on an exam. Scantrons and No. 2 pencils remind us all of late-night cramming.

While many might bristle at memorization-heavy course instruction, few think that it's a bad idea when it comes to learning math—especially multiplication tables and basic concrete facts about angles, formulas, and more. "You need that automaticity to build a foundation and go to the next step,"[4] argues Mary Mokris, senior advisor for Kumon, an education company. But there's research that suggests that even this can be taken too far. Educators looked at MRI scans of students with varying math memorization skills and concluded that "students are better at math when they've developed 'number sense,' or the ability to use numbers flexibly and understand their logic, which comes from relaxed, enjoyable, and exploratory work."[5] In other words, a focus on conceptual learning over mere memorization provides better foundational support to the student. "Drilling without understanding is harmful," said Jo Boaler, one of the researchers. "I'm not saying that math facts aren't important. I'm saying that math facts are best learned when we understand them and use them in different situations."[6]

The "pump and dump" approach to schooling a student—incentivizing the pretest "cramming" of information in one's mind for exam regurgitation, soon to forget most of it afterward—is certainly efficient but ultimately counterproductive. Learning content requires context; if we understand the "why," the "what" is easier to learn and remains longer in our minds. In a learning context, memorization "is almost always unnecessary for the student who thoroughly understands a few basic concepts. These students can then apply what they know to a broad range of problems and situations."[7] Even in a subject like math, there are a variety of formulas that "students try to memorize by reading them from a list over and over again. They commit these formulas to memory for just long enough to pass the test, then move on to whatever they need to memorize next. These students are doomed to repeat the process a year later when the topic comes up again. On the other hand, students who can relate all of these formulas to just a few well-understood facts and principles have very little to memorize and can apply what they know moving forward."[8]

When Caty DuDevoir was a student at a Portland high school, she—like so many of her peers across the country—was subjected to a barrage of standardized tests, each with multiple-choice questions that incentivize students to memorize and regurgitate basic facts and answers to perform well. She observed that teachers focused heavily on teaching information that would appear on a test, therefore reducing the quality of education she received. "I spend more time memorizing facts and equations rather than studying or learning the concepts,"[9] she admitted. That might be schooling, but it's certainly not learning.

Even if teachers aren't actively encouraging memorization and regurgitation, the structure of government schools and the nature of standardized tests can't help but incentivize it; students who want to perform well and get good grades find themselves pressured to cram information in their minds before an exam. In the aggregate, this approach to educating the rising generation yields a mediocre result because instead of challenging children to think critically and learn deeply, we bombard them with formulas and factoids to memorize and regurgitate.

OBEDIENCE TRAINING

A few years ago, an unsuspecting woman arrived at an eye clinic after seeing an advertisement for a free exam. She checked in and took a seat in the reception area, surrounded by a handful of people. While perusing one of the available magazines, she was startled by a loud beep from the overhead speaker. Suddenly, everyone seated nearby stood up and promptly sat back down. The woman's weirded-out glance revealed her discomfort with the situation—*what was going on?*

After the process repeated itself several times, the woman began acting the same as the others. Without having any clue as to what was going on, she stood up next time the beep sounded, doing what she thought was expected of her—then again, and again. For minutes, the beep prompted everyone to stand up and sit down. But then it got weirder. One by one, the other people were called into the doctor's office, ultimately leaving only the woman in the reception area. All alone, she continued to stand up for the beep, having no idea why.

As it turns out, this was an experiment set up by the TV show *Brain Games* on the *National Geographic* channel. Everyone was in on it except the woman; the people sitting nearby were all actors. It was a simple demonstration of social conditioning, showing the propensity of people to comply with what they are told to do or what they see others do. Numerous psychological studies indicate how most people will obey authority figures, most famously the Milgram experiment—which found that around two-thirds of individuals would administer progressively harsher electric shocks, even fatal ones, to another person if instructed to do so by the person in charge.

This tendency toward compliance is cultivated in government schools, where permission is required even to do something as essential as using the bathroom. "Everyone who has ever been to school," writes psychology professor Peter Gray, author of the book *Free to Learn*, "knows that school is prison, but almost nobody beyond school age says it is. It's not polite."[1] Children are compelled by law to attend these institutions, prohibited from voluntarily leaving, given orders on precisely what they should do at any given time, and required to obtain permission if they wish to do something different than the collective. Many school campuses now have a police presence, ostensibly to defend the children against a potential external threat, but inevitably degrading into further enforcement of school policies and state laws regarding student conduct. In Texas, for example, a study of twenty-two of the state's school districts found that over six years, school police had issued one thousand tickets to elementary school children as young as six.[2] What once was a reason to be sent to the principal's office can now land you in court with heavy fines or an even worse punishment.

Government schools are inherently prisonlike in their basic features and, therefore, prize obedience over most anything else. Fashioned after the Prussian militaristic model where youth were required to be obedient to orders without exception, American "factory schools" similarly inculcated the importance of strict rule following in the minds of students. John Dewey's early building of American schools was also heavily influenced by the Marxist model of compliance, which he repeatedly praised for its efforts of encouraging a "collective mentality" and a "new morality" for the rising generation.[3] The architects of today's school system wanted their "new social order,"[4] which as Dewey wrote, required "changing the conception of what constitutes education."[5] This meant creating compliant people who had to be "educated" away from their individualized upbringing while institutionalizing the obedience to many small things, so they could ensure obedience to the big things—whatever the collective required. This obedience training—the coordinated effort to "counteract" an "individualistic ideology" that naturally arose from family life and church influence—was "the great task of the school."[6] Social conformity was the true purpose—not academic achievement.

Parents enroll their children in government schools with the expectation they will be taught whatever is necessary to become competent adults. Few place their children in these institutions with the hope or understanding that they will be socially indoctrinated, their basic psychology leveraged in order to condition them into compliant individuals for the collective. And yet, that is the clear byproduct of these mediocre institutions. In the words of Johann Gottlieb Fichte—the philosophical father of the Prussian model of education, which became the blueprint for state schools in America and beyond—the purpose of schooling is "to be a reliable and deliberate art for fashioning"[7] children into model citizens for the state, "to which we shall first of all have to turn our expectant gaze."[8] Perhaps this is why academic outcomes for students in government schools are so persistently mediocre—it isn't the primary focus.

UNSAFE SCHOOLS

On May 24, 2022, an eighteen-year-old individual entered Robb Elementary School in Uvalde, Texas, and opened fire. In the school creating mayhem for more than an hour, the killer fatally shot nineteen students and two teachers, wounding seventeen others. Police officers were on the scene within three minutes of the shooting but did not intervene; nineteen officers "waited 74 minutes on-site before breaching the classroom to engage [the killer]."[1] An investigative report later concluded that the officers "failed to prioritize saving the lives of innocent victims over their own safety... there was an unacceptably long period of time before officers breached the classroom, neutralized the attacker, and began rescue efforts."[2]

These school shootings always attract substantial media interest, and for obvious reasons. No one likes to think of vulnerable children being made targets, like fish in a barrel. These fairly frequent incidents have prompted twenty states to allow teachers or school staff to carry firearms in the hopes that this might have a deterrent effect. And this may stand to reason since all school shootings have occurred in schools that don't allow them to carry:

> There has yet to be a single case of someone being wounded or killed from a shooting, let alone a mass public shooting, between 6 a.m. and midnight at a school that lets teachers carry guns. Fears of teachers carrying guns in terms of such problems as students obtaining teachers' guns have not occurred at all, and there was only one accidental discharge outside of school hours with no one [being] really harmed. While there have not been any problems at schools with armed teachers, the number of people killed at other schools has increased significantly – doubling between 2001 and 2008 versus 2009 and 2018.[3]

Many teachers can carry firearms in Texas, but not at schools in Uvalde, where this shooting occurred; the school board's policy incorporates federal law, stating, "It is unlawful for any individual knowingly to possess a firearm at a place that the individual knows, or has reasonable cause to believe, is a school zone."[4] Since President Bill Clinton signed the Gun Free Schools Act, which required states to pass "zero tolerance laws" for weapons possession by students, the federal government has showered states with funding for "school safety." Billions of dollars in funding has been spread across school districts countrywide, and yet "No evidence shows that this half-billion-dollar-per-year program has made schools any safer... Both the Office of Management and Budget and the Congressional Budget Office have tried to kill this program. Yet both Republican and Democratic presidents have joined with opposition parties in Congress to keep the program alive."[5] No politician wants to look like they aren't willing to "do whatever it takes," even if what they do is totally ineffective. Like with the TSA, the government's effort to fund "safe schools" is tantamount to security theater—metal detectors, police presence, backpack searches, and more still don't create a safe environment. Even worse, money is siphoned off for irrelevant activities:

> In Richmond, Virginia, where a ninth grader shot and wounded a basketball coach and a teacher's aide two days before school let out in June [1998], state education officials spent $16,000 to publish a drug-free party guide that recommends staging activities such as Jell-O wrestling and pageants "where guys dress up in women's wear," wrote the reporter, Ralph Frammolino. He also found that "taxpayer dollars paid for motivational speakers, puppet shows, tickets to Disneyland, resort weekends and a $6,500 toy police car. Federal funds also are

routinely spent on dunking booths, lifeguards and entertainers, including magicians, clowns and a Southern beauty queen, who serenades students with pop hits." In one of his most disturbing discoveries, he wrote that months before the middle school shooting in Jonesboro, Arkansas, by two adolescent boys, local officials used some of the safe-schools funding to hire a magician to perform in the school.[6]

School shootings certainly get a lot of attention, but the problem is far worse. A federal review of school safety found that there had been nearly a million violent incidents at US schools during the 2019-2020 school year.[7] Seventy percent of schools reported having at least one violent incident, prompting more than half of schools to have a police presence at least once a week.[8] In response to years of concerns about student safety, the entire system is changing:

Every day in communities across the United States, children and adolescents spend the majority of their waking hours in schools that increasingly have come to resemble places of detention more than places of learning. From metal detectors to drug tests, from increased policing to all-seeing electronic surveillance, the public schools of the twenty-first century reflect a society that has become fixated on crime, security, and violence... In a strange paradox that is so American, children are considered both potential victims, vulnerable to dangers from every corner, and perpetrators of great violence and mayhem, demanding strict, preventive discipline.[9]

Can students be inspired in such a setting? Does transforming the schoolhouse into a jailhouse full of "zero tolerance" rules cultivate curiosity and develop character? The answers are obvious. Not only are schools unsafe, but their transformation into security systems—and the prohibition on most teachers from arming themselves to eradicate these "gun free zones" that attract shooters—is counterproductive at best.

DUMBED DOWN CURRICULUM

In the days of *Little House on the Prairie*, it was common for children to drop out of school after the eighth grade—that was deemed enough required education before young people were able to get on with their lives. It was good to get some schooling, "but the cow needed milking and the field needed tending."[1] Advanced schooling was not particularly conducive to checking off one's chore checklist.

This was common enough throughout the United States that the phrase "only an eighth-grade education" fills family histories and biographies. After graduation, one's teen years were often spent working on the family farm—and for the boys, pursuing apprenticeships and early careers, or for the girls, helping run the household and preparing for marriage. When looking at this period of history, children were typically well disciplined and had good character—they learned to be industrious and had more responsibilities than children today. But at the same time, given their relative lack of education, we would consider an eighth-grade education woefully insufficient.

There's one problem with that characterization: the eighth grade of yesterday is not what it is today.

For example, consider the final exam given to eighth-grade students in Salina, Kansas, clear back in 1895. This five-hour test covered a wide variety of subject matter. For grammar, in addition to giving "nine rules for the use of Capital Letters" and naming "the Parts of Speech and defin[ing] those that have no modifications," students were told to "Write a composition of about 150 words and show therein that you understand the practical use of the rules of grammar."[2] Moving on to math, young students were required to "Name and define the Fundamental Rules of Arithmetic" as well as answer a variety of complicated questions such as:

> District No. 33 has a valuation of $35,000. What is the necessary levy to carry on a school seven months at $50 per month, and have $104 for incidentals?

> Find the interest of $512.60 for 8 months and 18 days at 7 percent.

> Find bank discount on $300 for 90 days (no grace) at 10 percent.[3]

And that was without a calculator or Google. For history, children were asked to "Relate the causes and results of the Revolutionary War," "Show the territorial growth of the United States," as well as describe prominent battles, events, and people.[4] And then there was orthography. (Do you know what that even is?) Students had to explain what elementary sounds are, diacritically mark a variety of words including their syllabication, and give four substitutes for caret 'u,' among many other questions. Finally, for geography, questions included:

> Name and locate the principal trade centers of the U.S.

> Upon what does climate depend?

> Name all the republics of Europe and give capital of each.

> Describe the movements of the earth. Give inclination of the earth.[5]

Fast forward a few years, and it wasn't any easier. An eighth-grade exam used in Bullitt County, Kentucky, in 1912 was similarly challenging. Arithmetic questions were difficult: "Find cost at 12.5 cents per square yard of kalsomining the walls of a room 20 feet long, 16 feet wide, and 9 feet high, deducting 1 door 8 feet by 4.5 feet and 2 windows 5 feet by 3.5 feet each."[6]

The grammar section asked: "What properties have verbs?" and "How many parts of speech are there?"[7] There were also sections on civil government, history, and physiology—where students were asked: "How does the liver compare in size with other glands in the human body? What does it secrete?"

Since 2007, the game show *Are You Smarter Than a Fifth Grader* has stumped countless contestants who did not know basic information found in fifth-grade textbooks. It's a comical show and a revelation regarding how useless to our adult lives so much of the content crammed into children's heads truly is. But the show only judges contestants based on modern schooling standards. How do you think anyone—whether an eighth grader today or an adult—would fare if they were asked some of the questions on these older tests?

By contrast, eighth graders today are held to a far lower educational standard—what some might call the "soft bigotry of low expectations."[8] The National Assessment of Educational Progress tests eighth graders on reading and math, asking such questions as: "The ratio of boys to girls to adults at a school party was 6 : 5 : 2. There were 78 people at the party. How many of them were adults?"[9] Or this one: "Tyler drinks 24 fluid ounces of milk each day for 7 days. How many quarts of milk does he drink in the 7 days?"[10] Most questions provide multiple choices for the answer. The reading section is full of doozies such as this one: "The author ends the essay with a childhood story. Does the childhood story do a better job persuading readers of the author's point than the other parts of the essay? Explain why or why not."[11] Mediocrity like this becomes far more apparent when compared against what was once expected of children of the same age.

One might argue that this dumbing down of government school standards was intentional—after all, why would those in power favor developing critical thinking and intellectual curiosity? People asking questions is an annoyance to the ruler who prefers obedience and ineptitude; it is easier to govern an ignorant population than an educated one. Perhaps for this reason, the critic H.L. Mencken once wrote:

> The most erroneous assumption is to the effect that the aim of public education is to fill the young of the species with knowledge and awaken their intelligence, and so make them fit to discharge the duties of citizenship in an enlightened and independent manner. Nothing could be further from the truth. The aim of public education is not to spread enlightenment at all; it is simply to reduce as many individuals as possible to the same safe level, to breed and

train a standardized citizenry, to put down dissent and originality. That is its aim in the United States, whatever the pretensions of politicians, pedagogues and other such mountebanks, and that is its aim everywhere else.[12]

Was he wrong?

A TOXIC ENVIRONMENT

As a freshman at Guilford High School in Connecticut in the fall of 2001, Jeremy Smith was unlike most boys his age. He stood only 4'7" and weighed seventy-five pounds. This presented a significant power imbalance between him and other boys at school, prompting many of his peers to bully him. He was pushed and shoved, picked up and cradled "like a baby" by bigger boys, verbally harassed daily, mocked with sexually suggestive comments, assaulted, restrained, and, on one occasion, forced into a backpack and paraded around school campus by a larger boy who wore him on his back.[1]

Jeremy's parents sued the school board seeking damages and reimbursement "for medical and psychiatric expenses for Jeremy's symptoms, including panic attacks, anxiety, a worsening of his attention-deficit disorder and post-traumatic stress disorder."[2] Where once Jeremy was a bright student with many friends, his grades fell, he lost weight, became depressed, and began resisting going to school. "I have never seen such a bright, happy child go downhill so fast in all my life," one of his teachers said.[3]

The lawsuit failed, and the school system was let off the hook. The judges cited "qualified immunity," a legal doctrine that shields government workers from being held accountable for wrongdoing. Warren W. Eginton, senior judge at the US District Court which dismissed the case, further argued that federal law "only requires that the state provide an appropriate education; it does not require that it be an optimal education."[4] In other words, the government offers only a mediocre education.

Roughly one-in-five government school students aged twelve to eighteen are bullied each year, according to a study by the US Government Accountability Office (GAO).[5] It is "especially prevalent in elementary and middle schools."[6] Over one million students each year are "bullied for their race, religion, national origin, disability, gender, or sexual orientation"[7]—a number that doesn't reveal the true breadth of the problem since children are also heavily bullied for their physical appearance, as in Jeremy's case, yet their statistics are not included in the GAO's list.

Bullying is too common in government schools—verbal (e.g., teasing, name-calling, threats), social (e.g., intentional exclusion, spreading rumors, embarrassing someone), and physical (e.g., hitting, pushing, damaging property). It has become worse in recent years as a result of the proliferation of technology, often turning what would have been a localized act of aggression into a "viral" one that spreads throughout the campus with children sharing photos, videos, and messages. A 2021 study assessing thousands of students aged twelve to seventeen found that the percentage of students who have experienced cyberbullying at some point in their lifetime has more than doubled from 18.8 percent in 2007 to 45.5 percent in 2021.[8]

Just as a prison often has infighting between inmates because there are a relatively few number of guards to monitor and intervene, government schools cannot ensure good behavior on the part of the countless students roaming the hallways or playing outside—where most bullying takes place. Research confirms the obvious: "The frequency and severity of bullying is inversely related to the degree of supervision present; that is, more, and more severe, bullying occurs where supervision is least."[9] In other words, children like Jeremy are easy targets for bullies in government schools where the students far outnumber the teachers and school administrators. And even when adults know about the bullying and fail to help prevent future situations, they cannot be held accountable by parents like Jeremy's since the courts routinely shield schools, like all government agencies, by giving them legal immunity for their misconduct.

The rampant bullying in government schools creates a toxic environment that stunts intellectual development. Jeremy's own experience in declining educational attainment is not an anomaly. A study of "over 3,500 elementary school students in 27 urban American schools found that bullying was linked to lowered academic achievement"—again confirming the obvious.[10] One mother described the transformation in her own daughter:

> The kids who bullied her would not let up and it was affecting her grades, her behavior, and her self-esteem. My child was once a happy student, always excited about going to school. She looked forward to learning and spending time with her friends, and doing the things that 12-year-olds do. But now, it was as if she was a completely different person. I was heartbroken. And the school was not being very cooperative, which also made me feel angry and helpless.[11]

It is difficult to be curious about and retain new ideas and information when you are being bullied; such harassment creates emotional distress and mental anguish that makes it very difficult for children to remain focused and interested in their studies.

In 1943, psychologist Abraham Maslow created a hierarchy of needs to describe human needs and behavioral motivation. Typically represented as a triangle, the base of the hierarchy is physiological needs—food, water, shelter, air, and so forth. From there, a person has basic safety needs—health, personal security, and emotional security. Once established, they can focus on social needs such as family and friendship. Only after these needs are all met are cognitive needs attainable, including self-actualization; one does not preoccupy oneself with the pursuit of esoteric knowledge when under attack by a predator. As such, it stands to reason that true and deep learning is likely not possible in an environment where students are so persistently subject to bullying by their peers. The education they do receive in such an environment will, thus, be mediocre at best.

A LINEAR MODEL

In 1914, writer Julian Street visited an automotive plant owned by Ford Motor Company. After walking the factory floor—soaking in sights and sounds that were altogether foreign to him—he wrote:

> Of course there was order in that place, of course there was... terrible "efficiency," but to my mind, unaccustomed to such things, the whole room, with its interminable aisles, its whirling shafts and wheels, its forest of roof-supporting posts and flapping, flying, leather belting, its endless rows of writhing machinery, its shrieking, hammering, and clatter, its smell of oil, its autumn haze of smoke, its savage-looking foreign population—to my mind it expressed but one thing and that was delirium.[1]

In the years prior to Street's visit, there had been initial attempts to experiment with assembly-line techniques, such as at Oldsmobile's factory in 1901 when workers "used wooden pallets outfitted with casters to roll automobile frames across its facilities."[2] Another used wooden dollies mounted with wheels to push the frames around between different workers. But it was Henry Ford and his team "who became most committed to the assembly line philosophy, and Ford Motor Company was the first to prove that assembly line techniques could be commercially viable."[3] The new process spread quickly:

> Management tweaked everything from the timing of its conveyor belts to the spacing between workstations in order to maximize efficiency. And within a matter of weeks, Ford began reaping enormous financial benefits, increasing production to an astounding 1,200 automobiles a day.[4]

As a result, "The assembly line turned the horseless carriage from a curiosity to a commodity; it cut the time necessary to build a chassis from fourteen hours to ninety-three minutes."[5] Efficiency indeed. And it was this precise level of control that education pioneers began implementing around the same time as it was spreading throughout the industrialized economy—the assembly lining of everything. It was Edward Thorndike and other advocates of "scientific management" who promoted the conveyor-belt methodology in schools. Their efforts were wildly successful.

> Following the model of the efficient factory, schools increasingly saw children as "raw ma-

terials" out of which they would fashion their "product"—productive adults. The apex of scientific management was manifest in the assembly line. One line might turn out Fords—to be sure, all running well and doing what Fords should do. Another line would turn out Lincolns—clearly a superior product. Managers did not value individual differences along the assembly line. Differences were defects in the product. So it has been with the school's scientific management ever since: individual difference within tracks often get labeled as flaws.[6]

As with an automobile or a smartphone or any number of complex products, students in government schools are treated as raw material that needs to be molded and modified at each progressive step. Each station requires the product to be fitted with the same parts (standardized curriculum) as all the other products proceeding down the same conveyor belt. If a product gets ahead, the worker slows it down to keep pace and maintain conformity. If a product falls behind, a "special" worker is assigned to help the product catch up. And after each station performs its task, the product receives a stamp of approval and is sent off for sale to the market.

This model of schooling—designed for an economy that is outdated by more than a century at this point—

organizes knowledge into a linear arrangement where tidbits of information are transferred into the minds of students in standardized formats and amounts. The teachers, for their part, are like technicians on the assembly line, ensuring consistency in the products and performing the same rote task for each new batch. The student is seen as a "blank"—as in the case of metal, where pressure is applied with a mold to create a new shape, consistent with all the others going through the process. Thus, these extremely outdated government schools require all children to learn the same things at the same time in the same way at the same age as everyone else. And yet, so few seem to question it:

> It is said that a fish is the last to find water. In other words, awareness of a certain aspect of reality is elusive when there is nothing else to compare it to. This aphorism is fitting to the way most of us think about school. Like the air we breathe, we take for granted that schools are organized into classes of students of the same age or with similar abilities, that classes are led by teachers, and that teaching involves telling students what to do and learn. We take for granted that curriculum is a body of information that is organized into a series of tasks that are systematically taught to achieve a stated objective. Despite the vast abundance of diversity in cul-

tural practices among the world's thousands of cultures, schools from around the globe share an uncanny sameness: desks are lined in rows where students sit facing teachers, recipients of knowledge. They listen, watch, observe, raise hands, and respond to teacher directives. And because much of the traditions and practices of school are so familiar as to be taken-for-granted, they are a challenge to change.[7]

The government school system, a "relic of the past,"[8] continues to this day using a conveyor-belt process designed to produce factory workers and human automatons in order to address social problems and economic circumstances that no longer exist. Could one design a more mediocre educational experience if they tried?

POOR PROBLEM SOLVING

Cathy Swift was a second-grade teacher in a large California school, tasked with implementing the state's new Mathematics Curriculum Framework in her class. She struggled to help her students learn all the assigned information, let alone the add-on concepts she was encouraged to teach, such as problem-solving skills. Asked by a supervisor why it was a challenge, Swift replied that the textbook and materials were fine enough, but the problems were too hard. Why?

> I don't know. They are not used to thinking, I guess. And it's really hard to teach although I do my best. And there isn't enough time to let them sit there and figure it out. I guess that's something I could use help with. I mean... how do you teach problem solving? But I don't know if anybody's come up with a great way to do it.[1]

While some teachers like Swift may struggle to teach problem-solving skills, other teachers are perplexed by how poorly students are actually doing. One high school teacher, sharing his concerns anonymously, articulated five points of frustration:

1. Students don't read instructions. I have no explanation for this. Even when I simplify my instructions into 7-8 word sentences, at least 1/3 of each class will skip over the instructions entirely, and 1/3 will misunderstand them. It's mind boggling.

2. Students seem to hate reading anything that's longer than one paragraph. Again, I have no explanation for this. When I assign a book, often giving generous time for students to read it, I'd say 1/3 of them won't ever open it and 1/3 of them will go to spark notes to get the gist, maybe reading a few chapters here and there that they think I'll ask about.

3. Students don't take feedback well. 2/3 of them ignore my feedback in its entirety. This 2/3 is usually the same group I mentioned in #2. They don't want to read, end up getting a bad grade, get mad at me for exposing their laziness, and then do nothing to improve it. However, I've noticed an uptick in decent students refusing feedback as well.

4. Students rush assignments, and then demand that I tell them "what to fix." This is kind of funny given point #3, in that even if I do tell them what to fix, they probably won't do it anyway. Lately, I give students examples of the quality I want, a rubric for them to see how the example scores well, and lots of opportunities to give feedback to each other's work. But they hate this system.

5. There's no enjoyment in learning. Learning is supposed to be enjoyed. Despite all of the differentiation strategies I put in place to create a classroom centered around this principle, students actively resist any enjoyment. Often, they can choose what text to read, how they want to connect this reading with their own lives, and how they want to present their knowledge. But they seem to hate this method just as much as a teacher-centered, full-on hour lecture. In other words, it doesn't seem to matter what strategy I employ to give their learning experience some joy, they all just kind of look at me and think, "no thanks."[2]

The reasons for such poor problem-solving skills among students are varied, but two primary influences have likely contributed to most of the problem. The first is the rise of standardized testing, accelerated as a result of the No Child Left Behind federal law. This method of testing educational performance requires measurable criteria, which means the data has to be quantifiable. These factoids, which help facilitate testing, are easily looked up and absorbed—only to be soon forgotten after the test is taken. And there is something important that this "growth in standardized test performance doesn't buy us: cognitive ability."[3] Filling out bubble sheets with a No. 2 pencil and becoming good test takers doesn't encourage the problem-solving skills that children need for their real lives.

The second major influence contributing to poor problem-solving skills is the immediacy of information as a result of ubiquitous technology access. When children are accustomed to searching for anything they need, they are trained to have others solve their problems for them. Conditioned to rely on outsourced information gathering, they learn the value of answers, not thinking. Clear back in 1989, a few years after *A Nation at Risk* was published, one researcher concluded that "three out of four U.S. students lack basic problem-solving skills" and that the country "has plenty of smart machines, but not enough smart, motivated people to put them to work."[4]

Some subjects lend themselves more easily to the development of problem-solving skills, such as mathematics or physics, where "clues are usually provided and there is an answer to the problem." But even with this foundation in school, "many students fail to apply and transfer the problem-solving skills learned in special subjects to problems in other subject domains and problems encountered in daily lives."[5] Government schools tend to "focus on forced recall of information" that "leaves children without the requisite skills to think through problems."[6]

"How do you teach problem solving?" Swift wondered out loud to her supervisor—a teacher whose job it was to do precisely that. Given their reliance on rote memorization and memory recall, schools are at best producing a mediocre result when it comes to encouraging problem-solving skills in today's youth.

CHASING THE WRONG GOALS

What do you want for your child? More important-ly, what do they want for themselves? These questions should influence how we educate our children, or en-list others to help us in that endeavor, yet few parents seem to think critically about the outcomes of school-ing—the goals being pursued by the system and its par-ticipants. It is like climbing a ladder to scale a building without first making sure it is placed on the right wall. If it isn't, then every step forward is a step in the wrong direction. Pausing to analyze offers us an opportunity to evaluate if the progress being made aligns with our goals.

What most parents truly want for their children cannot be assessed by a test or learned in a workbook. Parents want to raise children who are courageous, empathetic, innovative, resilient, motivated, curious, service-minded, persistent, and more. Then they place their children in an environment that not only does not exist to facilitate those goals but often inhibits them.

Imagine yourself twenty years from now. Any young children you have will be adults, pursuing a career and life outside of structured schooling. Imagine the type of people they will be—your conversations with them, the type of lives they lead, and your relationship with them. When you look back twenty years from now and reflect upon the education they received, will you be grateful they were forced to learn that the mitochondria are the powerhouses of the cell or "In fourteen hundred ninety two, Columbus sailed the ocean blue"? Will their schooling have adequately prepared them for the lives they are living two decades from now?

Good parents want to prepare their children for the future, equipped with the tools and training necessary to navigate their way through uncharted territory. But that preparation won't come by regurgitation or standardized examination. Government schools don't facilitate deep, meaningful learning about topics that students are individually passionate about—material that connects to their personal lives and the lives of others. With a reliance on structured, standardized curricula and by requiring conformity to it, these institutions don't support students in developing their unique interests and talents and cultivating them through engagement in project-based, applied learning. True education should inspire and elevate; it should enhance the individual instead of encouraging conformity. It should be a process of discovering and developing values that serve as a road map through your life, enhanced with the ability to think critically and act entrepreneurially, thereby responding to problems by bringing together resources and knowledge that will produce a solution. A root word of education—*educere*, in Latin—means to draw out, to lead out. It is a process of awakening and becoming, helping the student learn who they already are and can become. Instead of filling their minds with knowledge decided by someone else to be essential, it first focuses on the student and helps them discover themselves as they discover the world around them.

Erica Goldson, the high school valedictorian mentioned previously, shocked her teachers and school administrators by openly admitting how unprepared she was for life despite achieving a perfect academic record with extra credit piled on top. Her speech went viral and sparked conversation about how well (or poorly) schools are actually preparing children for their future lives. A few months after her speech, Goldson was asked to suggest three pieces of advice she would give to high school freshmen, who themselves are stepping into an unpredictable world. She offered the following:

> **1. Don't take school too seriously.** Sometimes that picture you're drawing is more important than studying for your Spanish test.

2. Get involved. Find your passions and explore them even more by joining or forming clubs.

3. Meet a lot of people. Learn as much as you can about what other people think and how little you actually know.[1]

Notice that she didn't emphasize getting good grades, completing all assigned homework, or making sure to thoroughly complete the curriculum. Her recommended goals were not the ones imposed on students in order to advance to the next grade or perform well on the SAT or ACT. Instead, Goldson's advice, if implemented, would lead students to pursue new experiences, new relationships, new perspectives, and an enriched sense of community and personal character—all things that parents desire in a well-rounded child primed for success in life. After all, the best lessons in life are typically not found in a classroom.

COMPETITION OVER COLLABORATION

Sometimes confessions are anonymous. That was the case with one high school graduate, a valedictorian, who revealed that he had cheated profusely throughout high school. "I was talented enough in my cheating to be mostly hailed as one of the smartest and most ambitious students in my graduating class," he revealed.[1] He explained his reasoning this way:

> It boils down to this: we are told that cheating is wrong because we are attempting to earn a grade that we do not deserve. A grade earned by cheating is not a grade reflective of our true achievement. But my contention uses identical reasoning. I cheated because the grade I would have otherwise been given was not reflective of my true learning.[2]

What is that "true learning" that the student was after, and for which he felt justified in skirting the expectations of the system he was enrolled in? "I felt cheated of the education I deserved," he wrote, "and thus to earn the grade I knew I deserved, I had to cheat the system."[3] It wasn't just him—his peers were in on it as well, and they also "knew that the classes they were attending were largely not adequately teaching them. And most of them went on to attend prestigious universities, majoring in the very fields they shamelessly cheated through in high school."[4]

At a surface level, a simple conclusion to draw is that the instructional model incentivizes cheating. The modern schooling model is such that teachers assess their students' ability to regurgitate information under examination rather than displaying mastery of a particular concept. In a system like this, a student might be motivated to take shortcuts once realizing the education is not substantive and personalized to the student's interests and future aspirations.

But there's something deeper that underlies the widespread acts of cheating in schools—where 74 percent of students report copying their friends' homework and 98 percent admitted to cheating in some capacity.[5] It is the structure of how children are being taught. Schools typically focus on individualized learning and discourage collaboration among students. This has led to a culture of isolation in the classroom, where students are taught to view their peers as competition rather than potential collaborators. This emphasis on individual achievement is often justified as a way to prevent cheating, but it ultimately does more harm than good.

One of the main problems with this approach is that it does not reflect the reality of the workplace. In the business world, collaboration is often the key to success. Companies rely on teams of employees to come together and work toward a common goal. In order to be successful in this environment, individuals must be able to work well with others and communicate effectively. Professionals "cheat" all the time, as it's commonly defined in schools. If they don't know the answer, they look it up. If they don't know how to do something, they ask someone else to show them. In a business environment, most decisions are jointly discussed and influenced by groups of peers; who happened to know a particular factoid or who completed a particular task is of little concern—the quality of the decision and the impact of the action is what matters. Employers want team players who can work well together, contribute to the goals, and discover the information they need along the way instead of individually knowing everything and working in isolation from others. If anything, "cheating" in work is actually rewarded—after all, why waste time reinventing the wheel when you can find the answers you're looking for elsewhere and move on to your next objective?

By contrast, students caught talking to each other during exams are yelled at or punished for cheating and made pariahs of the system for daring to run afoul of its expectations. Homework is designed as an individual activity, and students are disciplined if their work looks like anyone else's. From an early age, students are compelled to do their own work in isolation and view peers as competitors instead of collaborators. And while it is not entirely problematic to cultivate a sense of independence and self-reliance in young people, it must be balanced against the realities of life in which we as adults routinely share information, copy ideas, and use others' work to solve problems we have. Rugged individualism may have worked when children grew up to homestead their own property in isolation from neighbors, but this doesn't reflect the world today—yet government schools are still stuck in an antiquated model.

If schools are designed, in theory, to prepare children for their future lives and careers, one would expect that the model should regularly adapt to respond to changing socioeconomic circumstances in a developing society. Especially in the internet age of information abundance, it makes little sense to focus on memorization and regurgitation as the basis for learning. And since today's economy often requires collaboration and creative thinking among team members to achieve a desired result, it is counterproductive to punish students for acting as adults regularly do. Doing so leads them, like the anonymous student mentioned earlier, to see through the mediocre offering and respond by taking shortcuts to accelerate getting through it and moving on to something more rewarding and relevant.

NOT "COLLEGE READY"

On a rainy February morning in 2016, twenty students were huddled in a classroom working on mathematical word problems—but a few were stuck and couldn't make sense of the answer. One student raised her hand in confusion. "I got 1/10 as the answer, but the computer says it's 0.1," she reported.

"That's the decimal equivalent of 1/10, right?" the teacher asked in reply.

"I guess so," replied the girl.[1]

The teacher had to pause and use long division to explain how the two answers were the same, patiently taking time to go into enough detail for this girl and her peers to understand.

But this wasn't a young girl, and she wasn't in a middle school math class. This was a twenty-year-old college student struggling with basic math problems in a remedial class at Rutgers University-Newark. And this class isn't an anomaly—it is part of a broader trend that highlights how ill prepared many high school graduates are for college.

Approximately one-third of these graduates "require remedial or developmental work before entering college-level courses."[2] And the vast majority of higher education institutions report enrolling students like these—more than half a million of them, in fact—who are not ready for college-level work.[3] Hundreds of colleges placed *more than half* of incoming students in at least one remedial course.[4] And yet, the students themselves don't recognize their own educational deficiency; nearly 80 percent of students report believing they were "ready for college when they left high school," and the same percentage of students had a high school GPA of 3.0 or higher.[5] Clearly, there is a disconnect. Many of these students can't even handle the remedial classes: "Nearly 40 percent of students at two-year schools and a quarter of those at four-year schools failed to complete their remedial classes."[6]

Latasha Gandy got caught in the same trap. She was an ideal high school student in St. Paul, Minnesota who was focused on her studies and did all her homework. "I was that student everybody wanted to multiply," she said.[7] Gandy was in the honors program and graduated with a 4.2 GPA, but after getting substandard results on a placement test at a local community college, she was told she would have to take remedial classes. She didn't even know what remedial classes were, and she was surprised to learn she would need such classes since she had done so well in high school. She didn't understand how it was possible she wasn't ready for college.

Sadly, all of this comes at a very high cost. A study from the National Bureau for Economic Research found the annual cost of remedial education is about $7 billion.[8] And many of the students who are required to enter these classes "have a worse chance of eventually graduating than if they went straight into college-level classes,"[9] which suggests the need for a massive reconsideration of remedial classes in general.

But why is this done at all? The unfurling of the Common Core Standards in the wake of the No Child Left Behind federal law skyrocketed into popularity the term "college and career ready" as a goal for and descriptor of what government schools should be doing. Suddenly K-12 schools had a clearer focus—a rallying cry of sorts by which to benchmark their activities. The hope behind those pushing this program were summarized by then-secretary of education Arne Duncan who dreamed that "one day we can look a child in the eye at the age of eight or nine or ten and say, 'You are on track to be accepted and to succeed in a competitive university...'"[10] But this goal is fraught with difficulty since readiness is entirely subjective, highly individualized, and impossible to broadly measure:

> Does anybody possess a reliable, objective, measurable checklist that would allow us to declare with certainty that Pat is ready for college and Chris is not? Or that either is ready for any and all careers? Certainly a practiced eye can spot the extremes, the students who are very ready and those who are very unready. But that vast middle ground? Less clear.[11]

Imagine two high school seniors: one who wants to study marketing at a local community college and another who wants to study physics at Stanford. Is it reasonable to expect that both of these students should be similarly prepared for their totally distinct educational endeavors? Should someone studying philosophy at Princeton and someone else learning about business management at an online college really be required to read at the same level? With such varied educational pursuits and career tracks, the notion of college readiness is itself laughable, as there is no way to similarly prepare students who are going to be niching down into areas that require far more or far less preparation in certain subjects than other peers.

Jerome Cook is a principal at an Alabama high school who pinpointed the real problem underlying the growing remediation regime: "I don't think it's fair that some of these kids are leaving with As and Bs and then go into college and have to take remedial courses. I think they've dumbed down the curriculum trying to make sure students have good GPAs and test scores, and it's hurting these kids in the long run."[12] Mediocre curriculum standards and teaching methods have a cost, and it is one that many college students continue to pay for years after they get their diploma.

JUST-IN-CASE LEARNING

Think back to your own school years. Recall the many classes where you were lectured to by a teacher relying on a textbook designed around a structured curriculum through which you were being progressively led. In your science class, you were being coaxed into memorizing the various elements on the periodic table. In algebra you were having the quadratic formula and the Pythagorean theorem drilled into your head. In social studies, you were made to memorize the capital cities of all the states. Sometimes there were fun songs and mnemonic devices to help, but the overall approach was always the same: your mind was an empty vessel that had to be filled with knowledge—just in case you ever needed it.

Just in case.

In this teaching model, students are taught a broad range of information without necessarily understanding how that information will be useful to them in the future. They are expected to memorize facts and figures, but they are not given the tools to apply that knowledge to new situations or to solve real-world problems. The information they learn will be useful to them someday, they are told. Of course, that "someday" might be in a week or in two decades. It's a prediction that often fails to materialize for much of the content students are required to learn. This approach to learning is not only ineffective, but it can also be demotivating for students. When they are not given the opportunity to understand why they are learning certain information, they may lose interest in their studies and become disengaged. This can lead to a lack of motivation and a lack of curiosity, which can have negative effects on a student's overall education.

Just-in-case learning also leads to information overload—the perceived need to learn and be able to recall and apply all kinds of knowledge across a wide range of topics. Consider a business use case where this might apply. Imagine you need to assemble a vehicle—a complex system that includes hundreds of different parts. It would cause significant disruption to suddenly run out of a particular part, creating a bottleneck in the assembly line. So in response, a manufacturer might elect to warehouse massive quantities of each of these parts to maintain inventory just in case it's ever needed. And over the years, as new models are designed and new parts created, the manufacturer would have to keep on hand all of the prior parts just in case a customer's car needed one replaced. This massive inventory would be a beast to manage, and the problem would compound over time—similar to how a child's brain feels being crammed with information for thirteen years.

When he opened his manufacturing plant in Koromo, Japan, Kiichiro Toyoda developed a different method. For his new company, Toyota Motor Corporation, he and his associates pioneered a just-in-time approach:

> They invented a production system whereby the part that is needed is set to arrive exactly when it is ready to be distributed. The goal is to significantly decrease inventory that is lying dormant. The old method of having rows and rows of parts on a shelf in a warehouse is gone. Since Toyota began this program, it has been copied to some degree by a vast majority of major car suppliers.[1]

An education equivalent of the just-in-time model is to instead teach students how to problem solve and find information when they need it. Under this approach, students are given the tools and strategies to understand and apply new information, rather than just memorizing facts and figures. This approach emphasizes critical thinking and creativity, and it encourages students to take an active role in their own learning. One of its key benefits is that it better prepares students for the real world, where it is not enough to simply know a lot of information. Instead, students need to be able to adapt to new situations and use their knowledge and skills to solve problems and find new solutions. A just-in-time model helps students to develop these important skills, which are essential for success in the modern world.

Unfortunately, teachers are typically trapped in the just-in-case system. Government schools don't empower teachers to deviate from the highly regimented curriculum standards—they don't have much more say over what's being taught than their students do. And if a student were to raise her hand to ask why she is being required to learn the difference between cirrocumulus and stratus clouds, a teacher might honestly respond, "Because that is what the state mandates," or "Because that is what I am paid to teach you." If teachers aren't empowered to deviate from a top-down system, students will suffer.

COMPULSION

With waves of immigrants relocating to the United States of America in the mid-nineteenth century, many of the political and economic leaders of the time had grave concerns about the effects this mass migration would have. Still an emerging idea at the time, the tax-payer-funded "free schools" of the time were seen as a way to direct, assimilate, and control the new immigrants—to mold them into a homogenous "American" output that could better adapt and not disrupt the status quo. Immigrants were "expected to abandon their previous language, as well as their often contrasting and diverse values and cultures."[1]

In 1849, the president of Middlebury College, addressing the influential American Institute of Instruction, worried about the "multitude of emigrants from the old world, interfused among our population" who were "rapidly changing the identity of American character."[2] George Cheever, a well-known writer, put it more bluntly. He warned, "We are in great danger from the dark and stolid infidelity and vicious radicalism of

a large portion of the foreign immigrating population."
His proposed remedy was the government school:

> How can we reach the evil at its roots, applying
> a wise and conservative radicalism to defeat the
> working of that malignant, social, anti-Chris-
> tian poison? How can the children of such a
> population be reached, except in our free public
> schools?[3]

Horace Mann echoed these sentiments and thus
became a driving force in the formalization of government schooling to "inform and regulate the will of the
people."[4] However, strong encouragement for parents
to enroll their children in the free schools was insufficient—especially since many immigrants resisted
the idea. So where persuasion failed, Mann and his allies turned to force. In 1852, Massachusetts became
the first state to impose compulsory schooling by law
on children between the ages of eight and fourteen.
In An Act Concerning the Attendance of Children at
School, every city and town was required to have its
own school:

> The learning outposts needed to be equipped
> to teach math and grammar, and they differed
> from the ubiquitous church-run schools of the
> day because the clergy wasn't in charge. The
> law mandated kids between the ages of 8 and

14 years old be in a place of learning for at least three months a year and for at least six weeks in a row. Parents who didn't comply with the new rule were hit with a fine of up to $20.[5]

Other states quickly followed suit. By 1918, all states had passed compulsory education laws. Over time, these laws were expanded to require children to attend school for longer periods of time. By the mid-twentieth century, most states required attendance until the age of sixteen. In recent years, some states have raised the compulsory education age to eighteen. And while we typically think of compulsory education as a mandate for students and their parents to follow, teachers also became targets of early education reformers who succeeded in mandating that they enroll in state-approved teacher training courses as a prerequisite of employment in government schools. Eventually, teacher certification "came to be identified with the completion of teacher education programs rather than with the receipt of local certificates or the passing of subject-matter examinations."[6] The government's capture of education for both teachers and their students had created a closed loop.

Keep in mind that this was compulsory schooling, not necessarily compulsory *public* schooling. The government's position was that children must be in school, and that included the private schools that had proliferated, largely as a result of Catholic bishops encouraging parishes to start schools in response to the perception that the government schools were pushing a Protestant worldview. These bishops wanted to provide an alternative for Catholic parents who wanted their children to receive a religious education, but they were opposed by many elected officials who wanted to force children to attend government schools.

Consider the case of Oregon, where in 1922, voters passed the Compulsory Education Act via a ballot initiative which required children aged eight to sixteen to attend government schools for a certain number of days each year. The law was certainly controversial, as it was seen by many parents as an infringement on their parental rights to choose how to educate their children. Promoted initially by the Masonic Grand Lodge of Oregon as well as the Ku Klux Klan, the goal was to shut down religious schools in the state; only eight percent of the population at the time were Catholic.[7]

Naturally, Catholics were outraged—and they fought back. Spearheaded by Society of Sisters of the Holy Names of Jesus and Mary, the religious schools argued that the law "conflicts with the right of parents to choose schools where their children will receive appropriate mental and religious training, the right of the child to influence the parents' choice of a school, [and] the right of schools and teachers therein to engage in a useful business or profession."[8] The case was eventually heard by the US Supreme Court, which overturned the Oregon law, asserting that "the child is not the mere creature of the state."[9]

Even though the Supreme Court overturned compulsory *public* schooling, home education was still largely banned—children were compelled to be institutionalized one way or another. This was the case until the late 1970s when states began to relax their laws to allow parents to educate their own children. Homeschooling at the time was seen as a radical act that threatened the government's control over the education of children. In some states, homeschooling was considered a form of truancy, and parents could be held criminally responsible for not sending their children to school. In other states, homeschoolers were required to meet certain standards set by the local school district, such as providing evidence of academic progress or periodically submitting to tests. In a few states, homeschooling was still illegal until the early 2000s.

Compulsion is counterproductive to truly educating a child. Yet every state still threatens criminal charges and other punishments against parents who don't school their children to the state's satisfaction.

UNIONIZED MEDIOCRITY

Once gleaming as the Golden State, California is now a sad example of mediocrity in government schools. For example, the Los Angeles Unified School District is responsible for educating over 640,000 K-12 students, and yet is utterly failing. Fifty-two percent of the district schools earned a D or F in English language arts, and half of them earned a D or F in mathematics.[1] The teachers' unions in the district are largely to blame for this poor performance. These unions have spent years fighting for increased salaries for their members, regardless of the quality of instruction they provide. This has led to a system where teachers are paid more than they are worth and where administrators are unable to hold educators accountable for their performance. The result is a district that is overspending and underperforming.

The unions have also fought against the implementation of standardized tests and other measures of assessment that would help to identify and evaluate teachers. This has allowed mediocre teachers to remain in the system, while more effective educators leave for better opportunities. The public sector union is a type of labor union that represents workers in the government, including teachers in the public school system. These unions have significant power and influence in the government, and they have been able to dominate the public school system in many ways. And while Democrats are typically strong supporters of such unions, this was not always the case. For example, President Franklin D. Roosevelt was strenuously opposed to the unionization of government employees for purposes of demanding higher pay and more benefits:

> All Government employees should realize that the process of collective bargaining, as usually understood, cannot be transplanted into the public service. It has its distinct and insurmountable limitations when applied to public personnel management. The very nature and purposes of Government make it impossible for administrative officials to represent fully or to bind the employer in mutual discussions with Government employee organizations. The employer is the whole people, who speak by means of laws enacted by their representatives in Congress. Accordingly, administrative officials and employees alike are governed and guided, and in many instances restricted, by laws which es-

tablish policies, procedures, or rules in personnel matters.[2]

Teachers' unions dominate the government school
system through their ability to negotiate contracts
with the government—the so-called collective bargain-
ing that Roosevelt warned against. These contracts often include favorable provisions for union members,
such as higher salaries and better benefits. As a result,
teachers in the public school system are often paid
more than teachers in the private sector, even though
they may not be as effective in the classroom. This
disparity in pay can create resentment among private
sector workers and can lead to a decline in morale and
productivity.

Public sector unions also dominate the government
school system through their political power. These
unions are often well-organized and well-funded, and
they use their resources to support candidates who
are sympathetic to their cause. Consequently, they
are often negotiating for higher pay with people they
handpicked for office. As a result, many politicians are
beholden to the unions and are unwilling to challenge
their power and influence. This can make it difficult
for reform-minded policymakers to implement meaningful changes in government schools, thereby contributing to more mediocrity through simple inertia.

The domination of the government school system by public sector unions has also contributed to a lack of innovation and progress. Because the unions are able to protect their members from accountability, teachers in the public school system are often not incentivized to improve their performance or to try new methods of teaching. This leads to a stagnation in the quality of education and makes it difficult for students to learn the skills and knowledge needed to succeed in a changing economy.

Unionization is not inherently problematic. In the private sector, negotiations take place between a business owner and union representatives; two sides are represented, and opposing perspectives are worked through until a resolution is hopefully achieved. By contrast, in government,

> The citizens of the state who pay taxes and receive benefits are the stakeholders across the bargaining table from unions. The citizen stakeholders are represented by elected officials, most of whom have received significant campaign contributions from public sector unions. In such a situation, taxpayers are liable to exploitation by the union.[3]

In other words, there aren't two sides in the true sense—each party is benefiting from the same action—higher pay for (even poor-performing) teachers. Teachers get higher salaries and more perks, and politicians get campaign donations and reelection support. It's a win-win for the parties involved and a lose-lose for taxpayers and the children who this entire system exists to supposedly serve.

DIVERSE DISAGREEMENT

Stacy Dow struggled as a young student in the 1970s. Although intelligent, she was dyslexic and had trouble hearing and speaking. In second grade, she was doing so poorly in school that she was almost labeled as needing special education, something she says had "a very different and dismal meaning"[1] in those days. But her father decided to withdraw her from the local government school and found a different school that "focused on the whole child." She explains how much this helped her:

> It was exactly what I needed. I credit that one decision—to provide me with an opportunity to spend every day in an environment that was such a wonderful match for my strengths and weaknesses—with the fact that I was able to grow up with a love of learning, a Master's Degree, and a decent professional career. Things could have gone a very differently for me.[2]

Indeed, government schools struggle to accommodate the needs, interests and personalities of so many different children. It's something that Dow herself had to grapple with for her two daughters, who are both "twice exceptional"—someone who is both gifted and has a special need:

> I'll be honest and say that I've been worried about my options for public school. It has forced me to consider some very hard choices. I have very seriously considered relocating. Giving my children the opportunity to grow their whole selves, to foster all their creativity, to learn empathy and important social intelligence, to learn with context (project-based learning provides excellent context) rather than rote learning, to learn how to be good citizens; these things mean everything to me.[3]

One-size-fits-all systems are generally unable to produce good quality for a diverse range of inputs. Consider print-on-demand publishers that make it easy for authors to create physical books. This streamlined process is efficient and allows publishers to scale up the number of customers they serve, which is what they are optimized for. But to achieve this result, quality gets sacrificed; such systems typically offer a very limited set of options for paper type, book size, spine, and cover quality. Many authors are okay with that, but those wanting a high quality, professional product won't find it in such a system. Or consider cookie-cutter home builders who can pump out residential structures at a fast rate. To achieve scale and be efficient with time and cost, these builders provide prospective homeowners with a reduced selection of carpet types, cabinet styles, and room designs. By limiting options, they can build more homes more quickly. Again, many homeowners are okay with that, but those wanting a high quality, customized home won't be able to rely on this system.

It's no different with our children. A one-size-fits-all government school system is unable to produce exceptional educational performance for a diverse range of student abilities and interests. Yes, the system can scale—over 53 million children are enrolled in government schools.[4] And yes, it's efficient. But the result quality is not high. Many parents are apparently okay with that, but those wanting a high-quality education for their children cannot rely on a system like this. And the system itself cannot adapt to the diverse demands and desires of families, each of whom might disagree on how they want their children to be raised and educated.

The government school system is a product of the Industrial Revolution when standardization and uniformity were valued. The idea was that by providing a single, standard education for all children, the entire population would benefit. However, this system fails to take into account the needs of individual families. Parents may have different views on the importance of certain subjects or the need for extracurricular activities, and the government school system cannot meet these individual needs. Like with books and homes, so too with children—an efficient system that focuses on scale must sacrifice quality.

It is not uncommon for outspoken parents to show up at their local school board meeting and vocalize concerns over particular aspects of the curriculum standards, teaching methods, and content being used in the classroom. Oftentimes, these parents demand change, like when the Barrington School District removed honors-level classes in high school. One mom of two high schoolers, Shelly Edgar, was confused and upset. She wanted the change reversed. "This is the third year in a row that this has happened," she said, "where we get the program of studies, and there are significant changes to it without any dialogue or transparency."[5] Her reasoning for wanting parental input?

> Kids are different. They have different needs. We want them to be engaged learners who are excited about school, excited about making progress, and that means that they need to be met in unique ways.[6]

But the school system cannot adapt to accommodate that—and many people believe that is for the better. Brian Dickerson, editor of the *Detroit Free Press*, believes that this resistance to parental input—and the diversity of perspectives parents bring to the education of their children—is a feature, not a bug, of the system. "Parents aren't in charge of our public schools—and they shouldn't be," he wrote.[7] And everyone in the community, including childless strangers, has "every right to expect that the schools they subsidize with their tax dollars will prepare students to live and work in a democratic society that includes people with political and religious views different than their parents."[8] Parental control is pushed aside by a system that can't—and won't—accommodate it.

The government school system is a one-size-fits-all substandard system that will never be able to meet the diverse needs of individual families and their children. Parents may have different ideas about how to raise and educate their children, and the government school system does not provide the flexibility needed to accommodate these differing views. Those wanting something different for their children are compelled to look elsewhere.

NOT GOOD ENOUGH FOR THE ELITE

In the fall of 2019, Elizabeth Warren was on the campaign trail trying to boost her chances at securing the Democratic nomination for president. One of her stops was a historically black college in Atlanta where she was met by protesters from the Powerful Parent Network, a group of parents engaging with elected officials to make sure that they hear not just from professional teachers and their union bosses, "but hear from real parents whose children are being left behind generation after generation."[1] They assembled after growing tired of hollow promises from politicians for improvement in government schools, and members began advocating for alternative education options for their children besides the substandard schools in their local neighborhood.

A 2019 poll shows that two-thirds of African Americans support using taxpayer dollars for alternative schools,[2] yet Warren's platform proposed taking things in the opposite direction. In particular, Warren wanted to ban for-profit charter schools and end vouchers and tax-credit scholarships that allow low-income families who are unhappy with their public schools to send their children to private ones. A few of the protesting parents interrupted Warren's speech, demanding to be heard. "Our children, our choice!" they began chanting.

The exchange led to an opportunity to engage after the event where the parents and Warren had a lengthy discussion about the issue. One of the parents, Sarah Carpenter, told the presidential hopeful, "We are going to have the same choice that you had for your kids, because I read that your children went to private schools." Warren quietly responded, "No, my children went to public schools."[3] It was a lie. In fact, the senator's son, Alex, attended an expensive private school in the 1980s, meaning that Warren's claim was about as credible as the one about her Native American ancestry. The day after this event, Warren's campaign quietly confirmed that she had obfuscated the truth.

Politicians like Warren often claim that they want to help low-income families and minorities and improve the schools to better serve students' needs, yet they fight tooth and nail against any alternative options—competitive forces that would pressure the government's schools into actually improving. And the glaring double standard is also quite common—being in a financial position to send your children to a better school but denying the opportunity to those without the means to do so. It smacks of elitism and hypocrisy. It also shows what these elected officials actually believe. In economics, we call these *stated preferences* and *revealed preferences*. Put simply, what someone claims to be their belief or desire is their stated preference—what they are stating to be the case. But that person's actions—what they actually do—constitute their revealed preferences, revealing what they actually believe or desire. In Warren's case, she regularly reminded people on the campaign trail that she attended and taught at public schools. She bragged that she is "#PublicSchoolProud." Yet not proud enough, it seems, to stop her from exercising her school choice right by sending her child to an expensive private school while relatively few others have the means for their children to pursue educational excellence elsewhere.

This double standard betrays a deep-seated skepticism about the quality of government schools in the United States. It is a sign that these politicians feel schools are not providing the same quality of education as private alternatives—and they're not wrong. The evidence for this is overwhelming. According to the US Department of Education:

- Private school students generally perform higher than their public school counterparts on standardized achievement tests.

- Private high schools typically have more demanding graduation requirements than do public high schools.
- Private school graduates are more likely than their peers from public schools to have completed advanced-level courses in three academic subject areas.
- Private school students are more likely than public school students to complete a bachelor's or advanced degree by their mid-20s.[4]

Smaller class sizes and more supportive communities in alternative education settings often allow teachers to better connect with and support each child. This can help students discover and pursue their passions rather than getting lost in the crowd as they might in larger schools with hundreds or thousands of students. It is something that members of the Powerful Parent Network want for their children, but the politicians who claim to speak for them stubbornly refuse, instead insisting on propping up a failing institution because of the political benefits such support provides them, typically through campaign donations from teachers' unions that protect the status quo.

According to a recent survey from the Heritage Foundation, 44 percent of senators and 36 percent of House members in the US Congress "have sent a child to private school. That's 38 percent of lawmakers using private schools at some point. Nationwide, only a third—roughly 11 percent—of students attend private schools."[5] The opposition to school alternatives by elitists like Warren and her congressional colleagues is not only hypocritical, but it also denies low-income families the same opportunities for educational excellence that they provided for their children. By fighting against alternatives to traditional public schools, these politicians are actively working against the interests of the very people they claim to support.

Ultimately, it is clear that the opposition to creating competition to government schools is driven by self-interest and a desire to protect the government-run education system rather than a genuine concern for the education of all students. Instead of trying to block alternative education options, these politicians should be working to improve the quality of education and not propping up an expensive, mediocre system.

LOOKING TO THE PAST, NOT FUTURE

Despite significant advancements in technology and society over the past 150 years, the delivery of education has remained largely unchanged since the inception of government "factory" schools. Students are still expected to attend school in person, sit in a classroom with a teacher, and learn the core subjects of reading, writing, and math. In addition to these fundamental skills, schools are also expected to teach students how to be good citizens and prepare them for the challenges of adulthood. While there have been some attempts to modernize the education system, such as with the introduction of online learning and widespread standardized testing, the basic structure and goals of these schools have remained largely unchanged for over a century. This lack of innovation in government schools has left many students and parents frustrated as they struggle to adapt to a rapidly changing world.

This widespread discontent was captured in a national poll that found 96 percent of parents think students need to better develop skills to succeed in the twenty-first century. Of these, "64 percent said schools are not making these skills a priority," and only 24 percent of adults are happy with what is being taught in K-12 schools.[1] This indicates a major disconnect between the skills that schools prioritize and the skills that students actually need to succeed. It is clear that schools are failing to adequately prepare students for the challenges of the modern world—and parents realize it because they themselves were often ill prepared for the jobs they now have.

Today's economy is drastically different than it was when government schools were first designed. Despite this economic transformation of our society, government schools prepare students for a world that no longer exists. For example, the rote memorization and regurgitation of information is no longer applicable in a modern economy where the focus is on creative problem-solving, collaboration, and working with technology. Furthermore, schools don't focus on helping students develop skills such as communication, critical thinking, and the ability to work in teams—all of which are essential skills in the twenty-first century.

Beyond that, there are numerous skills that can empower people to thrive professionally in a fast-changing digital economy. Consider how artificial intelligence will render obsolete many occupations and tasks currently performed by humans, just as prior technologies and automation have done before. Where in government schools are students being taught things like computational thinking and data analysis? These are critical for people who may work alongside robots and AI. Perhaps for this reason, one-third of technology and education experts surveyed by the Pew Research Center felt that "education systems would not evolve enough within the next ten years to prepare workers for the jobs of the future."[2] Why does this system persist in training children with habits and knowledge that are not helpful as adults? As one education reformer wrote, this is a significant problem:

> It is hoped that students will learn to adapt to inevitable changes as well as becoming architects of their own future as they anticipate what they will need to know and be able to do later. Schools categorically fail to promote the development of a future context for students. They tend to be too enamored with the stock of knowledge ascertained in the past, which it is believed can simply be transmitted to children and successfully used by them, while ignoring the necessity of engaging students in forward-looking problem solving.[3]

That "future context" is essential to consider and closely related to a concept from psychology known as the "future self." This idea refers to the person you might imagine yourself to be at some point in the future. This future self can be thought of as a mental representation of who you hope to become or who you expect to become based on your current plans and actions. This concept can be helpful in making decisions and setting goals as it can provide a sense of direction and motivation. It can also be useful in considering the potential long-term consequences of your choices and actions. What about for your children? What do you anticipate their future selves to be? Mentally project yourself two decades into the future, considering who your child is and how they are living. If you could speak to that future version of your child and ask them about their schooling years, what might they say? Would they tell you that the knowledge they were taught and the training they received were relevant and useful to their lives? Or might they say, as do so many adults today, that extremely little of what they learned has any application in their adult years?

Government schools do not encourage this forward-looking thinking as it would be easily evident to most people participating in such a process that the conventional teaching methods used in government schools are largely ineffective—some might say mediocre—in preparing youth for today's world and quickly changing future. Put simply, a major overhaul of the system is necessary to ensure that the students who attend these schools are equipped with the skills they need to thrive in the modern economy.

LOCAL LACK OF CONTROL

World War II was coming to a halt in the early months of 1945. The Russians, pushing from the east, were pressing on the Germans and containing them to about 100 miles from Berlin. Poland was almost completely in Soviet hands. And after the Battle of the Bulge, Allied troops were pressing Germany from the west. Overseeing the plans was General Dwight Eisenhower, who intended to have the British advance on German forces west of the Rhine River. But General George Patton, overseeing some of the American forces, was frustrated with the apparent ineptitude and foot-dragging from the British. Despite being ordered to maintain an aggressive defense, Patton instead decided to wiggle around the command.

Patton's soldiers pushed forward with an armed reconnaissance of the German defenses—a sort of intentional provocation to allow them to push forward despite being in an aggressive defense. Eisenhower's office radioed Patton's army, ordering them to halt outside of the city of Trier because it "would take four divisions" to seize it.[1] Unbeknownst to the office, Trier was already in American hands as Patton's soldiers had pushed through with the infantry. On March 2, 1945, Patton radioed back to headquarters with a stinging reply: "Have taken Trier with two divisions... what do you want me to do, give it back?"[2]

Patton's independent approach to warfare was not without controversy, and he faced criticism for his aggressive tactics and outspoken personality. However, his success on the battlefield earned him the respect of his fellow commanders and the admiration of his troops. He sought forgiveness instead of begging for permission, and he utilized what autonomy he could muster to act as he saw best. This approach led him and his soldiers to several strategic victories.

That is the power of decentralized decision making—allowing people on the ground who best understand real-time conditions and changing circumstances to make the best, informed choices. Having disconnected and uninformed people making such significant decisions is a recipe for disaster—both on the battlefield and in the classroom. Instead of a top-down approach where a single authority makes all the decisions about how millions of children are educated, a decentralized schooling approach would allow teachers and other educators on the ground to make decisions that are best for their students and their specific circumstances. This would, quite obviously, lead to more effective and personalized teaching as educators would have the autonomy to adapt their methods to fit the needs of their students.

Instead, the hands of these educators are too often tied by state and federal mandates. A complex web of statutes restrict how government schools must operate. These governments, for example, all impose specific curriculum standards that schools must follow, limiting the ability of teachers to adapt their methods to the needs or interests of their students; the checklist of items becomes prioritized over pausing to pursue deep learning on topics of more relevance or interest. As a result of these laws, schools are subject to a variety of testing requirements in order to assess student performance. These tests often have specific pass rates that schools must meet; this limits, or eliminates, the flexibility given to teachers and incentivizes them to "teach to the test" so that they, in turn, receive favorable evaluations of their teaching performance by having students optimize for exam scores. And taxpayer-funded schools are made to follow specific funding formulas that allocate resources based on factors such as student enrollment rather than the specific needs of the school that may differ from what was decreed by those in charge of the budget at higher levels of government. This can prevent schools from investing in the resources and programs that would best support student learning.

No Child Left Behind, Common Core, and so many other national initiatives have made it clear that the idea of "local neighborhood schools" so often touted by teachers' unions and PTA members is a myth. These institutions are "now merely local outposts of a large, metastasized conglomerate controlled from the top, largely by unelected bureaucrats who elected representatives refuse to control."[3] This produces massive inefficiencies and waste—in both time and taxpayer treasure—by inhibiting innovation. By contrast, a decentralized education model that allows local schools to actually control their curriculum, structure, and budget would allow teachers and school administrators to make decisions that are best suited to their students and their specific circumstances. It would foster a sense of ownership and accountability among teachers (since they would no longer be mere disciplinarians and fact repeaters), surely leading to improved outcomes and a more positive learning environment for students. And it could foster innovation and experimentation in the school system as educators would have more autonomy to try new approaches and methods that differ from what some distant committee of faceless bureaucrats mandated. This could lead to the development of more effective and engaging teaching methods as well as a more dynamic, vibrant education system overall.

Patton's military success hinged in large part on his access to intelligence—being in the trenches, as it were—and his ability (or audacity) to act upon it. Educators deserve the same autonomy, yet are denied that flexibility in the government schooling system—to the detriment of millions of kids who are made to meander through mediocrity.

STUNTING THE GIFTED

When Caitlyn Singam was in kindergarten, her teacher suggested to her parents that she be labeled as a special-needs student because she was intellectually backward. This was a shock to her father, who noted that the young girl was already reading, including advanced material, at that young age. The teacher informed Singam's father that she "was finishing her reading assignments 'too fast' to have any understanding of the material."[1] When the dad suggested that his daughter might simply be an advanced reader, the teacher said, "she did not think it possible the girl could be so far ahead of her peers."[2] Although gifted, she was being branded as deficient.

As Singam got older, she faced significant resistance from school administrators when her parents inquired about moving her up a grade or two. According to the spokesman for the school district, they decided to rigidly follow established protocols and "simply wanted to ensure all her needs were met."[3] Never mind the fact that her needs were not being met by being held back to sit in a desk next to children who were similar in age but not ability. Singam recalled what his daughter's kindergarten teacher had warned him years before: "Public schools simply didn't have the means to support my daughter."[4]

When politicians and pundits discuss education reform, they typically highlight the perceived need for more funding and programs. Their attention focuses almost exclusively on children at the bottom of the pack—the underachievers and disadvantaged children struggling to keep up with teachers' lessons. And while this is a laudable goal when providing education broadly to millions of children, there is a lack of attention on the high achievers—a result of the "teaching-to-the-middle" tendency of most government schools. David Lubinski led a study at Vanderbilt University analyzing the relationship between top-performing children and future achievement. "Gifted children are a precious human-capital resource,"[5] he points out—and a severely underutilized one, since the government school system does not adequately support and challenge these students. The study focused on students scoring in the top 0.01 percentile on the SAT at a young age (or, in other words, those who ranked higher than 99.99 percent of their peers). And there was a problem they discovered: the students' early academic excellence was "belied by years of educational setbacks and systemic pitfalls."[6]

Another researcher on the project further highlighted the problem:

> There's this idea that gifted students don't really need any help. This study shows that's not the case. These people with very high IQs—what some have called the "scary smart"—will do well in regular classrooms, but they still won't meet their full potential unless they're given access to accelerated coursework, AP classes, and educational programs that place talented students with their intellectual peers.[7]

Singam's experience is not unique; many gifted students are not provided challenging, intellectual opportunities in government schools. Nearly 80 percent of teachers surveyed in 2008 agreed that "Getting underachieving students to reach proficiency has become so important that the needs of advanced students take a back seat."[8] The system forces gifted students to remain in a holding pattern while teachers perpetually focus on underachievers hoping they will catch up. It is a cruel punishment—a boring waiting game—that never ends for those who can excel if adequately challenged. Indeed, the Vanderbilt study found that "13-year-olds in the top 3 percent of math ability who took the project's fast-paced math classes were twice as likely to go into math or science careers than a similar group that didn't take the classes."[9] But if a gifted child's spark isn't maintained, then they look for stimulation elsewhere. Of the approximately one million school dropouts every year, nearly one out of ten earned mostly As.[10] The biggest reason for quitting, cited by those top-performing students, is boredom. And worse, gifted children sometimes develop coping strategies to better fit in with peers, intentionally hiding their intellectual gifts and stifling their strengths since they are not praised and cultivated by the system they are in. This can produce feelings of alienation, anxiety, and a sense of shame that is completely counterproductive to helping them pursue their potential, which is ostensibly the entire goal of the education system.

Yes, there's an achievement gap in schools, but administrators and teachers are only focusing on the bottom, thus ignoring—and weakening—the top. One researcher remarked, "You could make an argument that [these neglected high-achievers] merit the greatest investment, because they're going to be the greatest producers, based on their early academic achievement."[11] But that is increasingly at odds with the school system's priorities.

Consider California, the pedagogical petri dish whose educational experiments often trickle down to (or are forced upon) other states. In 2021, the state's Department of Education announced a new framework for math in K-12 government schools that would structurally discourage gifted students from pursuing accelerated classes to study advanced concepts. With supposed inequity as the driving concern, the department's lengthy framework fretted, as summarized by one commentator:

> Too many students are sorted into different math tracks based on their natural abilities, which leads some to take calculus by their senior year of high school while others don't make it past basic algebra. The department's solution is to prohibit any sorting until high school, keeping gifted kids in the same classrooms as their less mathematically inclined peers until at least grade nine.[12]

One is reminded of Winston Churchill telling the House of Commons in 1945, "The inherent virtue of socialism is the equal sharing of miseries."[13] Like in Ayn Rand's *Atlas Shrugged*, the moochers and government administrators despise those who excel and, thus, throw roadblocks in their path to retard their progress. Parents of gifted children should look to this school system with extreme suspicion, for it treats such students as an academic afterthought.

MEDICATING THE YOUNG, SECRETLY

Kathleen Cataford was a nurse at a middle school in Hartford, Connecticut, who noticed a concerning trend that she shared in a local Facebook group with parents:

> As a public school nurse, I have an 11yo female student on puberty blockers and a dozen identifying as non-binary, all but two keeping this as a secret from their parents with the help of teachers, [social workers] and school administration.
>
> Teachers and [social workers] are spending 37.5 hours a week influencing our children, not necessarily teaching our children what YOU think is being taught[1]

One parent reported Cataford to the school district for harboring and sharing "transphobic" views. The superintendent subsequently issued a statement condemning these views. "Hartford Public Schools strives to provide an inclusive environment where all students feel seen, valued, respected, and heard," the statement read.[2] The superintendent further added that "the values [Cataford's comments expressed] are totally inconsistent with what we stand for"[3]—and then fired her. The stated reason was that Cataford had shared private information about a student, violating confidentiality requirements. But this is not true; her Facebook post only referred to an eleven-year-old girl in general terms when describing the school's policy to conceal the gender dysphoria of students from their parents unless students wanted it told.[4] And because Hartford schools clearly have more than one eleven-year-old, it seems more likely administrators were upset with the fact that their concealment of information from parents was being made public. So the question is: do school staffers shield such information from parents? One journalist fought and failed to get the schools to give him a direct answer to the question:

> The publicist replied that school nurses don't administer medicine to students. But that was not one of the questions.

> Pressed, the publicist replied that school staff members encourage students to discuss their gender dysphoria with their parents. That wasn't responsive either.

Pressed again, the publicist said Hartford school staff members dealing with a student's gender dysphoria follow written guidance from the state Education Department. But exactly how has Hartford's school system construed that guidance in the context of the nurse's assertions? That is, are parents told or not? If not, why not?

The publicist again refused to answer. He also refused to facilitate a call to the superintendent so she might be questioned directly about school system policy and practice and the veracity of the nurse's assertions.[5]

This whistleblowing has led to revelations elsewhere in the country—each of them raising the question of just how prevalent the practice is if so much secrecy surrounds the issue. Consider the case of Anacostia High School in Washington, D.C., where out of around 450 students, only one percent are proficient in math and only four percent are proficient in English. There, the school nurse provides pregnancy and STD tests and prescribes various forms of birth control to minors. "I feel really good about the fact that we offer the full range of options," she told a reporter.[6] She doesn't just conduct tests and counsel students. "If a student decides she wants an IUD, [the nurse] can insert it on the spot. She can prescribe birth control pills and then hand the student a packet."[7] Despite parental consent typically being required for field trips, sex ed classes, and taking prescribed medication, children as young as thirteen are getting birth control pills without their parents ever being notified. In New York City, they at least notify parents up front about the possibility, telling them that nurses will dispense contraceptives without telling parents unless they preemptively opt out. This, of course, requires that parents actually receive and read the initial notice, which often does not occur. (Less than two percent of parents returned the opt-out form.[8])

The sinister promotion and provision of medication to students without explicit parental consent is extremely problematic. Among other reasons, it violates the parent's right to make medical decisions for their children. As minors, they remain under the care and custody of their legal guardian, and that individual needs to be informed about medication decisions. They have a deeper knowledge of the physical and mental health history of their child than a school nurse, and they have the natural right to intercede in such questions based on whatever their reasoning might be. This secrecy can also be seen as a form of discrimination against parents who may hold different beliefs or values about gender identity, abortion, and medical treatment more broadly.

For example, some parents may believe that gender identity is determined by biological sex, and they may not support the use of hormone therapy or other medical treatments to alter a child's gender expression. Other parents may have different religious or cultural beliefs about abortion and would prefer their sexually-active daughter, who becomes pregnant, places the child up for adoption to a loving family. By secretly encouraging or providing medical treatment to students without parental knowledge or consent, schools and their associated medical providers are effectively ignoring the beliefs and values of these parents and denying them the opportunity to participate in their child's medical care.

What is perhaps most concerning is the development of a precedent whereby school administrators can empower a child to potentially harm themselves in the name of medical care, all outside the purview of parents. Pushing medication of any kind onto children, to affirm their gender, reduce teen pregnancy, or for any other perceived medical or psychological need, is something that must involve parents. Sadly, parents are being left out of the conversation in some government schools, and the trend seems to indicate that more schools will be undermining parents in the years to come.

TOO BIG TO FAIL

In the late 2000s, the global economy was approaching a financial crisis. Many banks had made very risky investments and were now facing bankruptcy. But instead of allowing these banks to fail, the government decided to bail them out using taxpayer money, deeming them "too big to fail" for fear of the economic ripple effects that such a failure might produce. This approach rightly drew criticism, with free marketeers arguing that socializing economic risk (making everyone else pay for it) "comes at a great cost to the American economy by misallocating capital, inviting political manipulation and putting taxpayers on the hook" for a decision that "will surely be accompanied by adverse, unintended consequences."[1] Half a trillion dollars later, the critics were ignored, and the bad decisions of banks had been subsidized by taxpayers who had nothing to do with them. The idea of "too big to fail" had taken hold and codified the idea that the government should legitimize ineffectiveness in the name of perpetuating the status quo.

The same can be said of government schools. Education is a massive industry that, like the bailed-out banks, is permeated with bad decisions, poor management, and risk. Their status quo is largely protected through consistent and increased funding with institutionalized resistance to reform that would help taxpayers more appropriately allocate capital and reduce political manipulation. Instead, we continue funding mediocrity.

The idea of government schools being "too big to fail" might seem odd since there is evidence everywhere of the institution's consistent failure. But failure looks different when it is incremental, just like the proverbial frog in the pot of steadily boiling water—it is hard to see the destruction of a system when it looks like extremely slow decay. But the failure of this system exists, in part, because it is too big in two ways. First, government schools warehouse an exceedingly large number of children. Many schools have thousands of students attending,[2] leading schools to operate more like a corporation than a community. A young child spending hours daily among so many peers gets lost in the shuffle easily; the school becomes impersonal simply because of the structure needed to support so many students. The adults spend more and more time managing the system instead of caring for each individual.

A teacher or administrator interacting with hundreds or thousands of students a year obviously will struggle to get to know them in any meaningful way. When students and teachers are not connected on a personal level, it can lead to a lack of engagement that can make children feel like their education is not important. This can demotivate them and negatively impact their performance. Or consider a sports team at a typical high school where competition is fierce for a few coveted spots given the large student population. Those who make the cut feel invested in the team and school, but the rest might feel marginalized because their participation is denied—at best, they are relegated to being cheerleaders on the sidelines. Large schools simply cannot connect with each child in the way they truly need to be inspired and educated.

The second way that schools fail by being too big is the ratio of students to teachers in the classroom. In the 1980s, the Tennessee Student Teacher Achievement Ratio project studied the effects of class size on student achievement. The project randomly assigned students to either small classes (thirteen to seventeen students per teacher) or large classes (twenty-two to twenty-five students per teacher). Researchers found a "definite advantage for small classes in achievement,"[3] even in kindergarten. This confirms common sense because teachers who can spend more time with each student are able to tailor their teaching to each child's specific needs and interests, which improves learning outcomes. Small class sizes don't mean that teachers necessarily change what they are teaching per se, but their efficacy increases. Two challenges arise from this data: government schools' class sizes need to be much smaller, and reducing class size might lead to the hiring of ineffective teachers simply to meet the demand— something that would undermine the sought after increase in quality education.[4]

And just as government schools are structured to teach to the middle, making it harder for underachievers to keep up and for overachievers to be intellectually challenged, the schools are also structured to accommodate extroverts who have a "need for lots of stimulation."[5] Introverts who want an individual path, a quiet environment, and an ability to focus free of distraction, are deprived of what works best for them when forced into peer working groups and classes full of children and constant commotion. The ideal, as one journalist notes, "would be to establish arrangements that facilitate differentiated instruction for varying personality types, but this might be difficult in large classes with students of diverse levels of proficiency and motivation."[6] This is precisely the problem for a system tasked with schooling everyone. Government schools must, of necessity, be big, leading to general efficiency for the collective but mediocre outcomes for any particular individual—especially children whose personalities and interests don't align well.

Like with corrupt banks mismanaging their resources, government schools are not, in fact, too big to fail. Their status quo should not be preserved, nor their mediocrity subsidized by taxpayers. They should be allowed to face market pressures that will reform them for the better, reallocate capital toward its best uses, and find efficiencies that actually help each individual child instead of striving so hard to shore up a failing system.

CLASSROOM MISMANAGEMENT

Put a group of school teachers together and you will often find them swapping stories about student discipline and sharing classroom management techniques more than they are discussing anything academic. Many teachers vent online about dealing with unruly children and the challenges it produces. After all, many teachers are drawn to the profession out of an optimistic or altruistic desire to prepare young people for the future. Then the reality sets in about what the culture in government schools is like—compelling children who don't want to be there to sit at a desk daily under threat of punishment and often substituting for parents who delegate to this system the upbringing of their children, seeing it as a free babysitting service.

"This first month has been draining and exhausting due to [teaching] alone," one new teacher vented to her peers.[1] Adding classroom management on top of that "has just made it all so overwhelming."[2] Another teacher shared that managing children "is the biggest and most critical aspect of the job. Above curriculum [and] test scores."[3] Classroom management is "why we have teachers" at all, another said.[4] And a veteran teacher added, "I can tell you that as an early childhood educator classroom management is probably the bulk of what we do."[5] What were meant to be educational institutions have metamorphosed into second homes and juvenile detention centers. Teachers are effectively disciplinarians, focused on keeping the peace and enforcing arbitrary rules. Even the NEA argues that classroom management is "by far the most important aspect of a successful classroom."[6] Not inspirational teaching or academic excellence. Managing misbehavior.

Roxanna Elden is well aware of the struggles teachers face to juggle so many children and maintain a productive learning environment. She had wanted to be a teacher since high school and achieved her goal. Now teaching at a high school near Miami, Florida, she has seen many of her peers leave the profession; one in ten teachers quit by the end of their first year.[7] Her own worst day was in late October:

> Her students were acting up, so she assigned them a long list of math problems even though she knew homework shouldn't be given as a punishment. Later she realized it was Halloween and that she had most likely only ruined the night for the kids who would do the homework—the ones who had been behaving any-

way. It was the last straw: She broke down crying in her car.[8]

After more than a decade of teaching, Elden launched an email subscription for fellow teachers—what she calls a Disillusionment Power Pack—to regularly share motivational anecdotes and encouragement. Thousands of teachers now subscribe, and it all started with a simple message she shared: "It's okay for new teachers to cry in their cars."[9]

There is plenty of research indicating that "classroom organization and behavior management competencies significantly influence the persistence of new teachers in teaching careers," since "disruptive classroom behavior is a significant reason why teachers leave the profession."[10] And it makes sense—teachers can't really teach much, or teach well, if they have to focus their time and mental energy on rule enforcement and discipline. As the president of Columbia University's Teachers College said, "If a teacher can't manage a classroom, nothing they're going to do will be successful."[11]

One teacher, Zach Groshell, reported that his private school experience was a liability when he sought employment teaching in government schools. "They are worried that my experience in these schools... has made me ill-prepared to be successful in their contexts."[12] And what is that context? Classroom management. For example, Groshell highlighted that being a good teacher at a private school doesn't require:

- controlling students' entry into the classroom

- teaching students to walk in a straight line in the hallways, in silence

- teaching students how to pass papers

- modeling and practicing how to sit on the carpet or at their seats

- rewarding students individually with points, tickets, or tokens

- using group or whole school rewards, such as raffle drawings and pizza parties

- implementing a "one student at a time" bathroom policy[13]

Children attending private schools, and certainly those being homeschooled, are not subjected to these classroom management practices that distract from teaching, waste time, and create stress. Since class sizes are smaller (especially true for the homeschoolers), educators and children have more opportunity to bond. Teachers in these environments can adapt to the needs and interests of each student, and because there is a personal relationship, each child is disincentivized to cause trouble. Another reason government schools struggle with classroom management, by comparison, is that they receive all the students who don't value education and don't want to be there. This reduces the overall efficacy of the teacher since those students frequently cause a disruption to learning. If your child is curious and eager to learn, how well will they do in a classroom where the teacher has to constantly stop the lesson to deal with a few problem students? This perpetual distraction makes it challenging for the other students and degrades the classroom learning quality.

Having to deal with so much classroom management may also create a vicious cycle that reinforces a negative outcome; by focusing so much on discipline, educators and administrators may prioritize compliance and obedience over critical thinking and creativity. Compelling children to follow arbitrary rules such as raising their hand to use the pencil sharpener or bathroom may facilitate a peaceful environment in the short term, but over the long term it may undermine the character development of each of those children. All in all, the fact that government school teachers have to focus so much of their energy simply on managing misbehavior means, unsurprisingly, that the academic output becomes mediocre at best.

MONOPOLY

Since going public in 2004, Google has expanded its online presence by acquiring more than two hundred businesses. They bought YouTube, the largest video platform; DoubleClick, which distributes a large portion of the world's digital advertising; and Android, the operating system that powers 80 percent of smartphones worldwide. This massive expansion and dominant market position has raised a few eyebrows from critics who argue that the company is a monopoly as a result of their market share. Gary Reback, an antitrust lawyer, is one such critic. He is fighting Google much like he did Microsoft three decades ago when he got the Justice Department to sue the company. When asked whether he really thinks Google is a monopoly, he replied: "Oh, yes, of course Google's a monopoly. In fact they're a monopoly in several markets. They're a monopoly in search. They're a monopoly in search advertising."[1] Reback's arguments were echoed by the Federal Trade Commission, which recommended filing an antitrust lawsuit against the company. They similarly argued that Google "has strengthened its monopolies over search and search advertising."[2] In late 2020, the US Department of Justice filed a lawsuit against Google for "unlawfully maintaining a monopoly in general search services and search advertising."[3]

It is not uncommon for critics of large corporations to decry them as a monopoly, pointing out how such a heavy presence in the market allows them to deter competition, exploit employees, and hold customers captive. In Google's case, 81.5 percent of desktop users and almost 95 percent of mobile users utilize their search tool. Many find this concerning, again arguing about perceived monopolistic practices because of the company's ability to exercise significant control over how we consume information.

It is particularly odd that the individuals who espouse these views are often ardent defenders of government schools, which are guilty of everything they claim to oppose. Unlike Google or other large companies, these schools have guaranteed customers as a result of compulsory schooling laws and a constitutional mandate to exist and receive taxpayer funding. They, too, have huge market share of the country's student population—over 75 percent of students in government schools, and nearly 90 percent if you include charter schools (which are also funded and regulated by the government). And their market position, sanctioned by law, allows them to deter competition, exploit employees, and hold customers captive.

A true monopoly is one where individuals are denied decision-making power about their consumption decisions. This is not true of Google, Amazon, Facebook, or other large companies. While they possess significant market share, no one is compelled to use their services. And yet antitrust advocates tirelessly try to break up these large institutions out of a perception that they deprive consumers of more choice. Again, government schools are as guilty as any other institution, yet are spared the ire of the monopoly busters.

From an economic standpoint, monopolies can produce goods and services at a higher price and a lower quality than in a competitive market. Consider Amtrak, a government-owned corporation that operates most intercity passenger rail service in the United States. It is a monopoly for several reasons. First, it is the only provider of intercity passenger rail service in many parts of the country, giving it a significant degree of market power even if it had competition. Second, its competition is eliminated by various regulations that restrict the entry of other rail companies into the market. Third, it is heavily subsidized by the government, which provides it with a significant competitive advantage over potential private-sector competitors. And what is the quality of the service? Mediocre at best. The service is notoriously low quality, with frequent delays and cancellations. The old trains are in poor condition with no amenities like comfortable seating or on-board food and beverage service. The same mediocrity is seen with government schools.

As with any true monopoly, competition can cure the problem—empowering families to use their tax dollars to pursue superior alternatives. And that is precisely why teachers' unions and others in the system fight so fervidly against school choice legislation. But competition is likely the only way government schools will rise above the mediocrity of past decades. We have seen the lack of competition lead to complacency—schools not evolving to teach students the skills needed for success in the current economy. Competition would:

- Drive schools to improve their educational offerings and services in order to attract and retain students
- Motivate teachers to provide high-quality education to their students in order to keep their jobs
- Promote innovation and the development of new educational methods and technologies that align with the high-tech economy

It is not unreasonable to suggest that teachers, like all other workers, are influenced by incentives. When a school has a monopoly on its students, the incentive to produce excellence is diminished. And the absence of competition in education can lead to parents being viewed as a nuisance rather than valued clients who may seek alternatives if they are not satisfied. Naturally, no monopoly wants competition; the privileged position of the status quo is defended until the institution is forced to reform by external pressure. If we want to fix the current mediocrity, we have to dismantle the monopoly.

CONCLUSION

"School is a twelve-year jail sentence where bad habits are the only curriculum truly learned. I teach school and win awards doing it. I should know."[1]

So argued John Taylor Gatto, who for nearly thirty years taught in government schools in New York City. He tried repeatedly to innovate in the classroom, empowering children to learn what they wanted to rise above the mediocrity of the system. He struggled to do so, being constantly constricted by the many regulations imposed by the institution. But despite the challenge, it was evident to his peers that he was on to something—cultivating students' curiosities and helping them apply learning in their lives beyond the narrow focus on the next test. Indeed, Gatto was praised so much that he was named New York City Teacher of the Year in 1989 and 1990. The year after that, he received the same award, and then was also named New York State Teacher of the Year. Just after that school year concluded, on July 25, 1991, Gatto published an op-ed in *The Wall Street Journal* explaining that he was no longer willing "to hurt kids":

There isn't a right way to become educated;
there are as many ways as fingerprints. We don't
need state-certified teachers to make education
happen—that probably guarantees it won't.

How much more evidence is necessary? Good
schools don't need more money or a longer
year; they need real free-market choices, variety that speaks to every need and runs risks.
We don't need a national curriculum, or national testing either. Both initiatives arise from
ignorance of how people learn, or deliberate in-
difference to it.

I can't teach this way any longer. If you hear of
a job where I don't have to hurt kids to make a
living, let me know.[2]

What is especially interesting about Gatto is that he
wasn't arguing from privilege or as the result of dealing
with persnickety parents in some upper-class part of
the city. He taught in Harlem, at Booker T. Washington
Junior High. At the time, the school was ranked one
of the worst in the entire state. Its student population
was almost entirely Black and Latino students, all of
them underprivileged and poor, and only about a third
of them coming from intact families.[3] Gatto had a hard
time because, as he said, "In a school with poor kids,

the staff and administration become inured to their failures. They don't believe the kids can do anything."[4] The mediocrity had no apparent remedy. But Gatto's award-winning methods bucked the trend and made an impact. Here is what he shared during his acceptance speech for the 1990 Teacher of the Year award:

> A short time ago I took $70 and sent a twelve-year-old girl from my class, with her non-English speaking mother, on a bus down the New Jersey coast to take the police chief of Seabright to lunch and apologize for polluting his beach with a discarded Gatorade bottle. In exchange for this public apology, I had arranged with the police chief for the girl to have a one-day apprenticeship in small town police procedures. A few days later, two more of my twelve-year-old kids traveled alone from Harlem to West Thirty-first Street where they began an apprenticeship with a newspaper editor; later three of my kids found themselves in the middle of the Jersey swamps at six in the morning, studying the mind of a trucking company president as he dispatched eighteen-wheelers to Dallas, Chicago, and Los Angeles.
>
> Are these special children in a special program? Well, in one sense yes, but nobody knows about this program but myself and the kids. They're

just nice kids from central Harlem, bright and alert, but so badly schooled when they came to me that most of them couldn't add or subtract with any fluency. And not a single one knew the population of New York City or how far New York is from California.

Does that worry me? Of course; but I am confident that as they gain self-knowledge they'll also become self-teachers—and only self-teaching has any lasting value.[5]

Gatto quit because he couldn't succeed—his creativity and compassion for the students wasn't enough. He was operating within a failing institution that undermined his efforts. So he quit in order to write books and speak across the country, warning parents about just how problematic government schools had become. And this was only a few years after *A Nation at Risk* was published in 1983. Gatto didn't want more children to drown beneath the rising tide of mediocrity, so instead of teaching them how to tread water, he swam to shore and started throwing out lifesavers.

Having now read this book, you face two options. First, you can minimize or dismiss the forty examples we shared. After all, your local neighborhood school isn't part of the problem, right? The teachers there are lovely and work so hard—and your school board doesn't seem as bad as others. Surely things aren't *that* bad for the kids in *your* community. Perhaps this book has been too critical, straining at gnats to exaggerate the problem, all in the name of selling books. Maybe the authors even have an ulterior motive? These thoughts are a natural defense mechanism; when confronted with new information that challenges our beliefs, it can be difficult for us to accept it. This is because our beliefs help define who we are and form the basis of our identity. When our beliefs are challenged, it can feel like a threat to our sense of self. Additionally, it can be emotionally uncomfortable to change our beliefs, especially if they have been a part of our identity for a long time. So resisting the information in this book makes sense if your children attend government schools, as did you and your parents before you. Choosing to do things differently than they have been done before requires hard work, and who wants to bother with that anyway?

Another option is to heed the warnings and take action—muster up the courage and commitment to pursue superior alternatives that will be a better fit for each of your children while minimizing or eliminating the negative aspects of their school experience. It has never been easier to step off the government school conveyor belt and explore other paths. Whether you choose private schools, microschools, homeschool co-ops, online learning, tutoring, cloud-based classrooms, or another option in a quickly evolving landscape of education entrepreneurship, there are solutions out there for every child. But we said at the outset that this book would not be about solutions. Instead, we chose to highlight some problems in detail to make crystal clear that you should seek them out.

We also asked whether you felt that America's schools and the education landscape have materially improved in the past forty years since *A Nation at Risk* warned the public about the sorry state of government schools. We hope that after laying out as many examples as years that have passed since then, you agree with us that the answer is an emphatic no. Our future as a country depends on fixing this foundational problem, and conventional approaches to improvement won't work. We will not overcome mediocrity through more teacher training, more taxpayer dollars, or more testing and technology. Things are at the point where the best course of action is to do what Gatto did: stop telling kids to tread water and, instead, throw them a lifesaver.

The decision is yours, and the stakes are high—both for your family and for our country. What will you choose?

ENDNOTES

FOREWORD

1. "'It Just Isn't Working': PISA Test Scores Cast Doubt on U.S. Education Efforts," *The New York Times*, December 3, 2019, https://www.nytimes.com/2019/12/03/us/us-students-international-test-scores.html.

2. "From 0.13 GPA to future graduate, mom of Baltimore student says 'We did it'," ABC15 News, March 29, 2022, https://wpde.com/news/nation-world/from-013-gpa-to-future-graduate-mom-of-baltimore-student-says-we-did-it-augusta-fells-savage-grade-changing-padding-enrollment-project-baltimore.

3. "Baltimore City Schools: 41% of high school students earn below 1.0 GPA" Fox45 News, July 12, 2021, https://foxbaltimore.com/news/project-baltimore/baltimore-city-schools-41-of-high-school-students-earn-below-10-gpa.

4. "K-12 School Spending Up 4.7% in 2019 From Previous Year," United States Census Bureau, May 18, 2021, https://www.census.gov/library/stories/2021/05/united-states-spending-on-public-schools-in-2019-highest-since-2008.html

5. "Fast Facts," National Center for Education Statistics, accessed January 20, 2023, https://nces.ed.gov/fastfacts/display.asp?id=66.

6. "Courses Taken, Credits Earned, and Time to Degree: A First Look at the Postsecondary Transcripts of 2011–12 Beginning Postsecondary Students," Institute of Education Sciences, April 2020, https://nces.ed.gov/pubs2020/2020501.pdf.

7. "Study: Nearly 1 in 4 Students Fails Military Entrance Exam" Fox News, January 8, 2015, https://www.foxnews.com/us/study-nearly-1-in-4-students-fails-military-entrance-exam.

8. "Army announces creation of Future Soldier Preparatory Course," US Army, July 26, 2022, https://www.army.mil/article/258758.

INTRODUCTION

1. National Commission on Excellence in Education, *A Nation at Risk* (Washington, DC: U.S. Department of Education, 1983), 5.

2. "The 123s of School Choice," EdChoice, April 19, 2022, https://www.edchoice.org/research-library/?report=the-123s-of-school-choice-2/.

3. "Lake Michigan Is The Most Dangerous Lake In The Country, And Here's Why," The Travel, October 4, 2022, https://www.thetravel.com/is-lake-michigan-dangerous/.

4. "Rip tides, few lifeguards: Why drownings in the Great Lakes will likely remain high," *The Detroit News*, July 29, 2022, https://www.detroitnews.com/story/news/local/michigan/2022/07/30/why-great-lakes-drownings-will-likely-remain-high/10118128002/.

5. Ibid.

6. "Increasing remedial education in college shows pitfalls in higher graduation rates," *The Washington*

Examiner, June 6, 2018, https://www.washington-examiner.com/red-alert-politics/increasing-reme-dial-education-in-college-shows-pitfalls-in-higher-graduation-rates.

7. "American Schools Are Training Kids for a World That Doesn't Exist," *Wired*, October 17, 2014, https://www.wired.com/2014/10/on-learning-by-doing/.

SHUTTERED SCHOOLS, SLIPPING TEST SCORES

1. "'Nation's Report Card': Two Decades of Growth Wiped Out by Two Years of Pandemic," The74, September 1, 2022, https://www.the74million.org/article/nations-report-card-two-decades-of-growth-wiped-out-by-two-years-of-pandemic/.

2. Ibid.

3. Lawrence C. Stedman, "The NAEP Long-Term Trend Assessment: A Review of Its Transforma-tion, Use, and Findings," Paper Commissioned for the 20th Anniversary of the National Assessment Governing Board, March 2009, https://www.nagb.gov/content/dam/nagb/en/documents/who-we-are/20-anniversary/stedman-long-term-formatted.pdf.

4. Ibid.

5. Ibid.

6. Natalie Wexler, "Why I'm Not Writing About NAEP Reading And Math Scores," *Forbes*, October 25, 2022, https://www.forbes.com/sites/nataliewex-ler/2022/10/25/why-im-not-writing-about-naep-reading-and-math-scores/.

7. "Ignore NAEP. Better Yet, Abolish It," EducationWeek, June 6, 2022, https://

   www.edweek.org/teaching-learning/
   opinion-ignore-naep-better-yet-abolish-it/2022/06.

8.   "NAEP Scores Are a 'Critical Reality Check.' Kids
     Pay the Price If They Are Misinterpreted," Educa-
     tionWeek, October 26, 2022, https://www.edweek.
     org/leadership/opinion-naep-scores-a-critical-
     reality-check-kids-pay-the-price-if-they-are-misin-
     terpreted/2022/10.

9.   "NAEP Scores Are Down. Funding Is Up.
     Wait, Wut?," Edunomics, October 22, 2021,
     https://edunomicslab.org/2021/11/01/
     naep-scores-are-down-funding-is-up/.

10. Stedman, "The NAEP Long-Term Trend
     Assessment."

READING, WRITING, AND... GENDER IDENTITY?

1.   "September 2022 Times/Siena Poll: Cross-Tabs for
     All Respondents," *The New York Times*, Septem-
     ber 16, 2022, https://www.nytimes.com/interac-
     tive/2022/09/16/upshot/september-2022-times-
     siena-poll-crosstabs.html.

2.   "LEAKED: Teachers Reveal How They 'Stalk'
     Kids, Sideline Parents To Pull Middle Schoolers
     Into LGBT Groups," The Federalist, November
     18, 2021, https://thefederalist.com/2021/11/18/
     leaked-teachers-reveal-how-they-stalk-kids-
     sideline-parents-to-pull-middle-schoolers-
     into-lgbt-groups/?utm_source=wnd&utm_
     medium=wnd&utm_campaign=syndicated.

3.   "Gender identity lessons, banned in some
     schools, are rising in others," *The Washing-
     ton Post*, June 3, 2022, https://www.wash-

ingtonpost.com/education/2022/06/03/
schools-gender-identity-transgender-lessons/.

4. "WA schools intentionally, dangerously lie to parents about their child's 'identity'," 770KTTH, August 2, 2022, https://mynorthwest.com/3472466/
rantz-wa-schools-intentionally-dangerously-lie-to-parents-about-their-childs-identity/.

5. "Ohio school district tells teachers they don't have to inform parents of students' name, pronoun changes," Fox News, September 8, 2022, https://
www.foxnews.com/politics/ohio-school-district-tells-teachers-they-dont-have-to-inform-parents-students-name-pronoun-changes.

6. "Maryland advises teachers to hide gender identity issues from K-12 parents," *The Washington Times*, April 28, 2022, https://www.washingtontimes.
com/news/2022/apr/28/maryland-advises-teachers-hide-gender-identity-iss/.

7. Ibid.

8. "California mother claims teachers manipulated her daughter to change her gender identity," *New York Post*, January 24, 2022, https://nypost.
com/2022/01/24/mother-sues-teachers-for-brainwashing-student-to-identify-as-transgender/.

9. "A K-12 Sexuality Education Curriculum," Advocates for Youth, accessed October 26, 2022, https://3rs.org.

10. "Gender identity lessons...," *The Washington Post*.

11. "Radical gender theory has now made its way into more than 4,000 US schools," Fox News, August 23, 2022, https://www.foxnews.com/opinion/
radical-gender-theory-made-way-4000-us-schools.

12. Tweet by Christopher F. Rufio, Twitter, August 10, 2022, https://twitter.com/realchrisrufo/status/1557462533430480896.

13. Ibid.

14. "Elementary school teachers hide 'Gender and Sexuality' clubs from parents," Reality's Last Stand, May 13, 2022, https://www.realityslast-stand.com/p/elementary-school-teachers-hide-gender?triedSigningIn=true.

15. Ibid.

16. Fox News Poll, September 15, 2022, https://static.foxnews.com/foxnews.com/content/uploads/2022/09/Fox_September-9-12-2022_Complete_National_Topline_September-15-Release.pdf.

POOR PREPARATION FOR GRADUATES

1. "Can You Answer These Questions From the Original SAT?," *TIME*, June 20, 2016, https://time.com/4372031/sat-anniversary-original-questions-quiz/.

2. "Rivaling the SAT: A Brief History of the ACT and Why It Was Created," Best Colleges, August 15, 2022, https://www.bestcolleges.com/blog/history-of-act/.

3. "The Other One," *The New York Times*, November 10, 2022, https://www.nytimes.com/2002/11/10/education/the-other-one.html.

4. "ACT scores," National Center for Education Statistics, accessed October 29, 2022, https://nces.ed.gov/fastfacts/display.asp?id=897.

5. Ibid.

6. "Average ACT Scores Drop to Their Lowest Point in Three Decades," *Reason*, October 13, 2022, https://

    reason.com/2022/10/13/average-act-scores-drop-to-their-lowest-point-in-three-decades/.

7. Ibid.

8. *A Nation at Risk*, 5.

9. "U.S. High School Graduating Class Trends," ACT, accessed October 29, 2022, https://www.act.org/content/act/en/research/services-and-resources/data-and-visualization/grad-class-database-2022.html.

10. "Average ACT Scores...," *Reason*.

11. "Parents 2021 | Going Beyond the Headlines," Project Appleseed, December 8, 2021, https://www.projectappleseed.org/_files/ugd/842f93_a5c-86ca884014d498a940f84fe1bc5fd.pdf.

12. "U.S. High School...," ACT.

13. "Average ACT Score For the High School Class of 2022 Declines to Lowest Level in More Than 30 Years," ACT, October 12, 2022, https://leadership-blog.act.org/2022/10/GradClassRelease2022.html.

14. Ibid.

15. "Inside the vast national experiment in test-optional college admissions," NBC News, April 10, 2022, https://www.nbcnews.com/news/us-news/college-admissions-test-sat-act-rcna23574.

PASSIONATE PARENTS ARE DOMESTIC TERRORISTS?

1. "Parental involvement and students' academic achievement: a meta-analysis," Educational Psychology Review, 2001;13(1):1–22.

2. "Teachers Complain of Lack of Parent Support," Associated Press, December 12, 1988, https://www.nytimes.com/1988/12/12/us/teachers-complain-of-lack-of-parent-support.html.

3. Ibid.

4. "Majority of Primary School Teachers Say Parents Don't Understand The Importance of Classroom, Teacher Engagement," Higher Ed Dive, June 24, 2019, https://www.highereddive.com/press-release/20190624-majority-of-primary-school-teachers-say-parents-dont-understand-the-import/.

5. "Woke Teachers Vs. Parents," *The American Conservative*, August 9, 2020, https://www.theamericanconservative.com/woke-teachers-vs-parents-matthew-r-kay/.

6. "Scottsdale Unified School Board Shuts Down Parents, Describes Them As 'Mob'," AZ Free News, May 20, 2021, https://azfreenews.com/2021/05/scottsdale-unified-school-board-shuts-down-parents/.

7. "Full NSBA Letter to Biden Administration and Department of Justice Memo," Parents Defending Education, November 29, 2021, https://defending-ed.org/press-releases/full-nsba-letter-to-biden-administration-and-department-of-justice-memo/.

8. "White House in contact with school board group for 'weeks' before controversial 'Patriot Act' letter: emails," Fox News, October 21, 2021, https://www.foxnews.com/politics/white-house-national-school-board-association-letter-emails-show. See also "National School Boards Association Admits to Colluding with Biden Administration on 'Domestic Terrorism' Letter," Breitbart News, May 20, 2022, https://www.breitbart.com/politics/2022/05/20/national-school-boards-association-admits-col-luding-biden-administration-domestic-terrorism-letter/.

9. "NSBA letter drafts called for National Guard and military to be deployed," Fox News, May 23, 2022, https://www.foxnews.com/media/nsba-letter-called-national-guard-military-deployed?intcmp=tw_fnc.

10. "Garland calls in FBI to counter reported threats against school staffers," *New York Post*, October 5, 2021, https://nypost.com/2021/10/05/merrick-garland-calls-in-fbi-to-counter-threats-against-school-staffers/.

11. "National School Boards Association Apologizes for Letter to Biden Admin Comparing Parents to Domestic Terrorists," CBN News, October 23, 2021, https://www1.cbn.com/cbnnews/us/2021/october/national-school-boards-association-apologizes-for-letter-to-biden-admin-comparing-parents-to-domestic-terrorists.

12. "National School Boards Association stumbles into politics and is blasted apart," *The Washington Post*, January 13, 2022, https://www.washingtonpost.com/education/2022/01/13/school-board-association-domestic-terrorism/.

BROKEN OR WORKING AS INTENDED?

1. Jo Ann Boydston, ed., *The Early Works of John Dewey, vol 5* (Carbondale: Southern Illinois University Press, 2008), 95.

2. Jo Ann Boydston, ed., *The Later Works of John Dewey, vol. 3* (Carbondale: Southern Illinois University Press, 2008), 230.

3. Ibid., 409.

4. "The Public School Curriculum," A. A. S. A. Official Report, *Including a Record of the Annual Convention*, 1934.

FLUSH WITH CASH AND FLUSHING CASH

1. "International Studies of Educational Achievement," SpringerLink, accessed October 29, 2022, https://link.springer.com/chapter/10.1007/978-94-010-0309-4_53.
2. "Poor U.S. Math Showing Didn't Surprise Experts," The Washington Post, March 12, 1967.
3. National Research Council, *STEM Integration in K-12 Education: Status, Prospects, and an Agenda for Research* (Washington, DC: National Academies Press, 2014), 1.
4. Ibid., 16.
5. Ibid., 17.
6. "What 2018 PISA international rankings tell us about U.S. schools," The Hechinger Report, December 16, 2019, https://hechingerreport.org/what-2018-pisa-international-rankings-tell-us-about-u-s-schools/.
7. Ibid., emphasis added.
8. "The U.S. Must Improve K-12 STEM Education for All," National Science Board, accessed October 29, 2022, https://www.nsf.gov/nsb/sei/one-pagers/K-12-Indicator-2022.pdf.
9. "Education Expenditures by Country," National Center for Education Statistics, May 2022, https://nces.ed.gov/programs/coe/indicator/cmd/education-expenditures-by-country. The PISA assessment comprises some 79 countries, 38 of which are members of the Organization for Economic Cooperation

and Development (OECD) which sponsors PISA. The amount spent by other countries referenced her pertains only to OECD member nations.

10. "Addressing the Critics of This Purportedly No Good, Very Bad Chart," Cato Institute, September 29, 2014, https://www.cato.org/blog/addressing-critics-purportedly-no-good-very-bad-chart.

11. Corey DeAngelis, "Washington Post didn't mention that real public school funding per student increased by 152% since 1970.," Twitter, May 7, 2022, https://twitter.com/DeAngelisCorey/status/1522928504249241601.

12. Corey DeAngelis, "Latest national data on growth in administrative staff, principals, teachers, and students in public schools (since 2000)," Twitter, May 7, 2022, https://twitter.com/DeAngelisCorey/status/1522934266912514051.

13. "Uneducated: Why American Education is Fundamentally Flawed," The Heartland Institute, January 8, 2019, https://www.heartland.org/news-opinion/news/uneducated-why-american-education-is-fundamentally-flawed.

14. "2020 Public Elementary-Secondary Education Finance Data," United States Census Bureau, Summary Tables, Table 11, accessed October 30, 2022, https://www.census.gov/data/tables/2020/econ/school-finances/secondary-education-finance.html.

15. Ibid.

16. "Follow the money: How schools spent their billions in COVID-19 relief funds," *Washington Examiner*, August 17, 2022, https://www.washingtonexaminer.com/restoring-america/community-family/follow-the-money-how-schools-spent-their-billions-in-covid-19-relief-funds.

17. "The Problem With Public Schools," Discovery Institute, August 25, 2021, https://www.discovery.org/education/2021/08/25/the-problem-with-public-schools/.
18. Ibid.
19. Ibid.

SCHOOLS: A JOBS PROGRAM FOR ADULTS

1. "Can Twitter Become More Profitable Under Elon Musk?," Barrons, April 26, 2022, https://www.barrons.com/news/can-twitter-become-more-profitable-under-elon-musk-01650998108.
2. "Twitter slashes nearly half its workforce as Musk admits 'massive drop' in revenue," *The Guardian*, November 4, 2022, https://www.theguardian.com/technology/2022/nov/04/twitter-layoffs-elon-musk-revenue-drop.
3. "Twitter Investors Decide To Ignore Drop In Quarterly Profit," *Forbes*, February 10, 2022, https://www.forbes.com/sites/abrambrown/2022/02/10/twitter-fourth-quarter-earnings/.
4. "There seem to be 10 people 'managing' for every one person coding," Elon Musk, Twitter, October 30, 2022, https://twitter.com/elonmusk/status/1586686935518498816.
5. "Growth in Administrative Staff, Assistant Principals Far Outpaces Teacher Hiring," *Education Next*, Vol. 22, No. 3, https://www.educationnext.org/growth-administrative-staff-assistant-principals-far-outpaces-teacher-hiring/.
6. "Friedman Foundation Takes a Critical Look at Administrative Bloat in Public Schools," The Daily Signal, October 24, 2012, https://www.dailysignal.

com/2012/10/24/friedman-foundation-takes-a-critical-look-at-administrative-bloat-in-public-schools/.

7. "Administrative bloat isn't the biggest problem facing school district budgets," Reason Foundation, November 29, 2021, https://reason.org/commentary/administrative-bloat-isnt-the-biggest-problem-facing-school-district-budgets/."

8. "The ongoing layoff process is a complete farce and an embarrassment," til, Twitter, October 30, 2022, https://twitter.com/taylorleese/status/1586936748181196800.

9. "New Study Makes Case For Fundamental Shift in Teacher Pay Systems," Texas Public Policy Foundation, July 11, 2000, https://www.texaspolicy.com/press/new-study-makes-case-for-fundamental-shift-in-teacher-pay-systems.

CIRCUMVENTING CURRICULUM RESTRICTIONS

1. "Williamson County Parents Warn Critical Race Theory Has Already Entered Their Public School System," *The Tennessee Star*, April 22, 2021, https://tennesseestar.com/2021/04/22/williamson-county-parents-warn-critical-race-theory-has-already-entered-their-public-school-system/.

2. Ibid.

3. Richard Delgado, *Critical Race Theory* (New York: New York University Press, 2017), 3.

4. "New York Times corrects The 1619 Project—but it's still a giant lie," *The New York Post*, March 14, 2020, https://nypost.com/2020/03/14/new-york-times-corrects-the-1619-project-but-its-still-a-giant-lie/.

5.   "Critical Race Theory in the Mathematics Classroom," The Activist History Review, December 15, 2021, https://activisthistory.com/2021/12/15/critical-race-theory-in-the-mathematics-classroom/.

6.   "Head of teachers union says critical race theory isn't taught in schools, vows to defend 'honest history'," CBS News, July 8, 2021, https://www.cbsnews.com/news/critical-race-theory-teachers-union-honest-history/.

7.   "We Checked, And They're Right; CRT Is Not Being Taught In Schools (Technically)," Daily Caller, July 29, 2021, https://dailycaller.com/2021/07/29/critical-race-theory-law-school-antiracism/.

8.   Ibid.

9.   "Teacher Anti-CRT Bills Coast To Coast: A State By State Guide," Forbes, February 16, 2022, https://www.forbes.com/sites/petergreene/2022/02/16/teacher-anti-crt-bills-coast-to-coast-a-state-by-state-guide/.

10. "Largest Teachers' Union Erases Campaign to Push Critical Race Theory from Website," National Review, July 6, 2021, https://www.nationalreview.com/news/largest-teachers-union-erases-campaign-to-push-critical-race-theory-from-website/.

11. "Iowa Governor Signs Law Banning Some Concepts Related To Racism, Sexism, From Diversity Trainings, School Lessons," Iowa Public Radio, June 8, 2021, https://www.iowapublicradio.org/state-government-news/2021-06-08/iowa-governor-signs-law-banning-some-concepts-related-to-racism-sexism-from-diversity-trainings-school-lessons.

12. "Video: Iowa Educators Admit That They Flout The State's Critical Race Theory Ban," Daily Caller, April

20, 2022, https://dailycaller.com/2022/04/20/iowa-educators-critical-race-theory-ban/.

13. Ibid.

14. "'Social and emotional learning' is often just cover for progressive indoctrination of kids," *New York Post*, November 23, 2021, https://nypost.com/2021/11/23/social-and-emotional-learning-is-often-cover-for-progressive-indoctrination/.

15. "Idaho school officials discuss bypassing state CRT ban in undercover video," *Washington Examiner*, March 23, 2022, https://www.washingtonexaminer.com/policy/education/idaho-school-officials-discuss-bypassing-state-crt-ban-in-undercover-video.

16. "School Administrators 'Worm Around' Laws Banning Critical Race Theory, Undercover Videos Reveal," *National Review*, March 25, 2022, https://www.nationalreview.com/news/school-administrators-worm-around-laws-banning-critical-race-theory-undercover-videos-reveal/.

17. "Accuracy in Media President Adam Guillette Uncovers Teachers Still Teaching Critical Race Theory in Public Schools Regardless of Law," *The Tennessee Star*, March 30, 2022, https://tennesseestar.com/2022/03/30/accuracy-in-media-president-adam-guillette-uncovers-teachers-still-teaching-critical-race-theory-in-public-schools-regardless-of-law/.

POLITICS › EDUCATION

1. "Military Brass, Judges Among Professions at New Image Lows," Gallup, January 12, 2022, https://news.gallup.com/poll/388649/military-brass-judges-among-professions-new-image-lows.aspx.

2. "Confidence in U.S. Institutions Down; Average at New Low," Gallup, July 5, 2022, https://news.gallup.com/poll/394283/confidence-institutions-down-average-new-low.aspx.

3. "Confidence in Institutions," Gallup, accessed October 31, 2022, https://news.gallup.com/poll/1597/Confidence-Institutions.aspx.

4. "'Never seen it this bad': America faces catastrophic teacher shortage," *The Washington Post*, August 3, 2022, https://www.washingtonpost.com/education/2022/08/03/school-teacher-shortage/?itid=ap_hannahnatanson.

5. National Education Association, accessed October 31, 2022, https://www.nea.org.

6. "2019 NEA Representative Assembly," Utah Education Association, accessed October 31, 2022, https://myuea.org/2019-nea-representative-assembly/.

7. Ibid.

8. Corey DeAngelis, "Just this morning their website still showed this 2019 resolution they DEFEATED calling to 'make student learning the priority of the Association.'," Twitter, July 6, 2021, https://twitter.com/DeAngelisCorey/status/1412498451686907906.

9. "NEA Embraces the Woke Agenda—but Votes down 'student Learning'," American Enterprise Institute, July 11, 2019, https://www.aei.org/education/k-12-schooling/nea-embraces-the-woke-agenda-but-votes-down-student-learning/.

10. "American Federation of Teachers," Open Secrets, accessed October 31, 2022, https://www.opensecrets.org/orgs/american-federation-of-teachers/totals?id=D000000083.

11. "National Education Assn," Open Secrets, accessed October 31, 2022, https://www.opensecrets.org/orgs/national-education-assn/totals?id=D000000064.

12. "Former NEA General Counsel: NEA is effective not because it cares about children, but because it has 'power'," Americans for Fair Treatment, December 17, 2021, https://americansforfairtreatment.org/2021/12/17/former-nea-general-counsel-nea-is-effective-not-because-it-cares-about-children-but-because-it-has-power/.

13. Ibid.

14. Ibid.

INFORMATION OVER INQUIRY

1. Ben Orlin, "When Memorization Gets in the Way of Learning," *The Atlantic*, September 9, 2013, http://www.theatlantic.com/education/archive/2013/09/when-memorization-gets-in-the-way-of-learning/279425/.

2. Scott Santens, "Stop Teaching Students What to Think. Teach Them How to Think," EducationWeek, September 26, 2017, https://www.edweek.org/education/opinion-stop-teaching-students-what-to-think-teach-them-how-to-think/2017/09.

3. Orlin, "When Memorization Gets in the Way of Learning."

4. "Cram. Memorize. Regurgitate. Forget.," Everyday Sociology Blog, April 26, 2012, http://www.everyday- sociologyblog.com/2012/04/cram-memorize-regurgitate-forget.html.

STUDENTS TREATED AS POLITICAL PAWNS

1.   Corey A. DeAngelis and Christos Makridis, "Are School Reopening Decisions Related to Union Influence?," *Social Science Quarterly*, March 25, 2021, https://onlinelibrary.wiley.com/doi/abs/10.1111/ssqu.12955.

2.   Michael T. Hartney and Leslie K. Finger, "Politics, Markets, and Pandemics: Public Education's Response to COVID-19," *Perspectives on Politics*, vol. 20, no. 2, 2022, pp. 457–473., doi:10.1017/S1537592721000955.

3.   Ibid.

4.   "Collection of 130 COVID Studies Aims to Give Schools a 'Solid Grounding' to Reopen," The74, March 11, 2011, https://www.the74million.org/collection-of-130-covid-studies-aims-to-give-schools-a-solid-grounding-to-reopen/.

5.   "Powerful teachers union influenced CDC on school reopenings, emails show," *The New York Post*, May 1, 2021, https://nypost.com/2021/05/01/teachers-union-collaborated-with-cdc-on-school-reopening-emails/.

6.   "White House considered teachers unions' labor disputes before releasing reopening guidance, emails show," Fox News, December 17, 2021, https://www.foxnews.com/politics/white-house-teachers-unions-labor-disputes-school-reopening-guidance-emails.

7.   "Teachers Unions Want Wealth Taxes, Charter School Bans, and Medicare for All Before Schools Can Reopen," Reason, July 28, 2020, https://reason.com/2020/07/28/teachers-unions-want-wealth-

taxes-charter-school-bans-and-medicaid-for-all-before-schools-can-reopen/.

8. Ibid.

TEACHER KNOWS BEST?

1. "Nevada mom goes viral after school board cuts her mic during meeting," *The Washington Times*, May 18, 2022, https://www.washingtontimes.com/news/2022/may/18/nevada-mom-goes-viral-after-school-board-cuts-her-/.

2. Ibid.

3. "Georgia parent reading sexual content from library at school board meeting is cut off: 'Inappropriate'," Fox News, March 24, 2022, https://www.foxnews.com/us/parent-reading-sexual-content-school-cut-off-board-member-irony.

4. Ibid.

5. Ibid.

6. "New Jersey teachers union condemns parents as 'extremist' in new ad," *The New York Post*, August 18, 2022, https://nypost.com/2022/08/18/new-jersey-teachers-union-condemns-parents-as-extremist-in-new-ad/.

7. "Please tell me what I'm missing here.," Eric Swalwell, Twitter, November 9, 2022, https://twitter.com/RepSwalwell/status/1590545381641060352.

8. "Educators love their students and know better than anyone what they need to learn and to thrive.," NEA, Twitter, November 12, 2022, https://twitter.com/NEAToday/status/1591587398109929473; emphasis added.

9. "Teachers union plays clean up after claiming educators 'know better than anyone' what kids need,"

Fox News, November 14, 2022, https://www.foxnews.com/media/teachers-union-plays-clean-after-claiming-educators-know-better-anyone-kids-need.

10. Fox News, "President Biden, first lady hosts the 2022 national and state teachers of the year," April 27, 2022, https://www.youtube.com/watch?v=JmoWVdmW1g0.

11. "MSNBC: We Have to Break Through This Idea 'That Kids Belong to Their Parents'," CNS News, April 8, 2013, https://www.cnsnews.com/news/article/msnbc-we-have-break-through-idea-kids-belong-their-parents; emphasis added.

SEXUAL ABUSE, AGAIN AND AGAIN

1. "Beard honored before Round Lake tops Libertyville," *Daily Herald*, October 5, 2013, https://www.dailyherald.com/article/20131005/sports/710059769/.

2. "Ex-Soccer Coach Pleads Guilty, Gets 6 Years For Sex With Students," Patch, October 27, 2018, https://patch.com/illinois/vernonhills/ex-soccer-coach-pleads-guilty-gets-6-years-sex-students.

3. Ibid.

4. "Notorious teacher sex scandals," CBS News, March 14, 2018, https://www.cbsnews.com/pictures/notorious-teacher-sex-scandals/.

5. "At least 269 K-12 educators arrested on child sex crimes in first 9 months of this year," Fox News, October 14, 2022, https://www.foxnews.com/politics/at-least-269-k-12-educators-arrested-child-sex-crimes-first-9-months-year.

6.   "How the Boston Globe exposed the abuse scandal that rocked the Catholic church," *The Guardian*, April 21, 2010, https://www. theguardian.com/world/2010/apr/21/ boston-globe-abuse-scandal-catholic.

7.   "Catholic Church sexual abuse cases," Wikipedia, accessed November 17, 2022, https://en.wikipedia. org/wiki/Catholic_Church_sexual_abuse_cases.

8.   "Educator Sexual Misconduct: A Synthesis of Existing Literature," Policy and Program Studies Service, U.S. Department of Education, Doc #2004-09, accessed November 17, 2022, https://files.eric. ed.gov/fulltext/ED483143.pdf.

9.   "At least 269 K-12 educators arrested on child sex crimes in first 9 months of this year," Fox News.

10. "Hidden horror of school sex assaults revealed by AP," Associated Press, May 1, 2017, https://www. ap.org/explore/schoolhouse-sex-assault/hidden-horror-of-school-sex-assaults-revealed-by-ap.html.

11. Ibid.

12. Ibid.

13. Ibid.

14. "R.I. teachers unions, ACLU object to bill criminalizing sex between school employees and students," *The Providence Journal*, April 9, 2019, https:// www.providencejournal.com/story/news/educa-tion/2019/04/09/ri-teachers-unions-aclu-object-to-bill-criminalizing-sex-between-school-employ-ees-and-students/5472189007/.

MO' BUREAUCRACY, MO' MEDIOCRITY

1.   "Not Another Test... The Right Test," *The Imaginative Conservative*, March 13, 2017, https://theimagi-

nativeconservative.org/2017/03/classic-learning-test-jeremy-tate.html.

2. "The first time I heard somebody say the Department of Ed should not exist I thought they were nuts.," Jeremy Wayne Tate, Twitter, March 28, 2022, https://twitter.com/JeremyTate41/status/1508604869384585220.

3. "United States Department of Education," Wikipedia, accessed November 17, 2022, https://en.wikipedia.org/wiki/United_States_Department_of_Education.

4. The Education of Shirley Mount Hufstedler," *The Wall Street Journal*, January 27, 1980, https://www.washingtonpost.com/archive/lifestyle/1980/01/27/the-education-of-shirley-mount-hufstedler/53577ec5-9548-4ac4-86d5-ffa9f0bd60b6/.

5. "Why Do We Have a Department of Education? Jimmy Carter's Debt to a Teachers Union.," Reason, February 7, 2017, https://reason.com/2017/02/07/department-of-education-jimmy-carter/.

6. Ibid.

7. "Movement to Abolish the Education Department, Decades in the Making, Lives On," Epoch Times, October 11, 2022, https://www.theepochtimes.com/movement-to-abolish-the-education-department-decades-in-the-making-lives-on_4691563.html.

8. Ibid.

9. Ibid.

10. "United States Department of Education," Wikipedia.

11. "Movement to Abolish the Education Department, Decades in the Making, Lives On," Epoch Times.

12. "US Secretary Of Education Miguel Cardona 'Standing With Educators;' DeSantis Standing Firm On Masks," CBS, August 13, 2021, https://www.cbsnews.com/miami/news/mask-mandates-educators-desantis/.

SOPHISTICATED SCHOOL SEGREGATION

1. Horace Mann, *Annual Reports of the Secretary of the Board of Education of Massachusetts for the Years 1845-1848* (Boston: Lee and Shepard Publishers, 1891), 251.

2. "50-State Review," Education Commission of the United States, March 2016, https://files.eric.ed.gov/fulltext/ED564952.pdf.

3. Ibid.

4. Ibid.

5. "FYI, Alabama's constitution still calls for 'separate schools for white and colored children'," *The Washington Post*, March 10, 2017, https://www.washingtonpost.com/news/answer-sheet/wp/2017/03/10/fyi-alabamas-constitution-still-calls-for-separate-schools-for-white-and-colored-children/.

6. "How early SF kept Chinese children out of the schoolhouse," *The San Francisco Chronicle*, April 15, 2017, https://www.sfchronicle.com/bayarea/article/How-early-SF-kept-Chinese-children-out-of-the-11074408.php.

7. Tim DeRoche, *A Fine Line: How Most American Kids Are Kept Out of the Best Public Schools* (Los Angeles: Redtail Press, 2020), back cover.

8. "The U.S. student population is more diverse, but schools are still highly segre-

gated," NPR, July 14, 2022, https://www.
npr.org/2022/07/14/1111060299/
school-segregation-report.

9. Ibid.

10. Ibid.

CONFORMITY OVER CURIOSITY

1. "Here I Stand," America Via Erica, June 25, 2010,
    http://americaviaerica.blogspot.com/p/speech.
    html.

2. Ibid.

3. "'Schools are killing curiosity': why we need
    to stop telling children to shut up and learn,"
    The Guardian, January 28, 2020, https://www.
    theguardian.com/education/2020/jan/28/
    schools-killing-curiosity-learn.

4. Ibid.

5. Ibid.

TEACHING TO THE TEST

1. "Why I Will Not Teach to the Test," Edu-
    cationWeek, November 12, 2010, https://
    www.edweek.org/teaching-learning/
    opinion-why-i-will-not-teach-to-the-test/2010/11.

2. "Teachers march against 'teach to the test'," People's
    World, June 10, 2013, https://peoplesworld.org/
    article/teachers-march-against-teach-to-the-test/.

3. "Why I Will Not Teach to the Test,"
    EducationWeek.

4. "Leaving creativity behind / Drilling for tests kills
    curiosity and imagination," SFGate, March 12, 2006,
    https://www.sfgate.com/education/article/Leav-

ing-creativity-behind-Drilling-for-tests-2539779.
php.

5. "Ocean Springs Middle School students get party for top test scores," Gulf Life, February 24, 2012, https://www.gulflive. com/mississippi-press-living/2012/02/ ocean_springs_middle_school_st.html.

6. "Parental Rights in Public Education Amendments," Senate Bill 204, 2015 General Session, https:// le.utah.gov/~2015/bills/static/SB0204.html.

7. "Atlanta Cheating: 178 Teachers and Administrators Changed Answers to Increase Test Scores," ABC News, July 6, 2011, https://abcnews. go.com/US/atlanta-cheating-178-teachers-administrators-changed-answers-increase/ story?id=14013113.

8. "Better Tests Don't Lead to Better Teaching, Study Finds," U.S. News and World Report, November 13, 2017, https://www.usnews.com/news/national-news/articles/2017-11-13/better-tests-dont-lead-to-better-teaching-study-finds.

9. Lorrie Shepard, "Measuring Achievement: What Does It Mean To Test for Robust Understanding?," Educational Testing Service, accessed November 19, 2022, https://eric.ed.gov/?id=ED415238.

10. Robin Harwick, "Teaching to the Test Harms Students," Medium, October 5, 2020, https://medium.com/the-faculty/ teaching-to-the-test-harms-students-5f9752e0c9bf.

THE YOUNGER, THE BETTER

1. "Lawmakers approve measure making kindergarten mandatory," *The Buffalo News*, June 18, 2014,

https://buffalonews.com/news/local/lawmakers-approve-measure-making-kindergarten-mandatory/article_73575414-956e-5d01-9cb7-dcf749f9f5e4.html.

2. Ibid.

3. Ibid.

4. Ibid.

5. "50-State Comparison: State K-3 Policies," Education Commission of the United States, accessed November 20, 2022, https://www.ecs.org/kindergarten-policies/.

6. "Free, State-Run Preschool Worse for Poor Kids Than No Preschool, Study Finds," Reason, February 16, 2022, https://reason.com/2022/02/16/tennessee-pre-kindergarten-study-worse-for-kids/.

7. Ibid.

8. Ibid.

9. "Words of Friederich Froebel," Froebel Web, accessed November 20, 2022, https://www.froebel-web.org/web7001.html.

10. Peter Gray, "Research Reveals Long-Term Harm of State Pre-K Program," Psychology Today, January 31, 2022, https://www.psychologytoday.com/us/blog/freedom-learn/202201/research-reveals-long-term-harm-state-pre-k-program.

11. "Experts: Half-day kindergarten a 'disaster'," *The Philadelphia Inquirer*, May 1, 2011, https://www.inquirer.com/philly/education/20110501_Experts__Half-day_kindergarten_a__disaster_.html.

12. "Mandatory Kindergarten Won't Be Coming to California," Reason, October 5, 2022, https://reason.com/2022/10/05/mandatory-kindergarten-wont-be-coming-to-california/.

PUMP AND DUMP

1. "The Roles of Memorization in Teaching & Learning," EducationWeek, July 29, 2020, https://www.edweek.org/teaching-learning/opinion-the-roles-of-memorization-in-teaching-learning/2020/07.
2. Ibid.
3. Ibid.
4. "Should we stop making kids memorize times tables?," The Hechinger Report, February 9, 2015, https://hechingerreport.org/should-we-stop-making-kids-memorize-times-tables/.
5. "Math and the brain: Memorization is overrated, says education expert," Stanford Medicine, February 3, 2015, https://scopeblog.stanford.edu/2015/02/03/math-and-the-brain-memorization-is-overrated-says-education-expert/.
6. "Should we stop making kids memorize times tables?," The Hechinger Report.
7. "'Memorization Often Comes Without Understanding'," EducationWeek, July 30, 2020, https://www.edweek.org/teaching-learning/opinion-memorization-often-comes-without-understanding/2020/07.
8. Ibid.
9. "It's Not a Memory Test; Education Needs to Focus on Critical Thinking," Maine Public, June 8, 2018, https://www.mainepublic.org/maine/2018-06-08/its-not-a-memory-test-education-needs-to-focus-on-critical-thinking.

OBEDIENCE TRAINING

1. Peter Gray, *Free to Learn: Why Unleashing the Instinct to Play Will Make Our Children Happier, More*

   Self-Reliant, and Better Students for Life (New York: Basic Books, 2013), 67.

2. "Texas school police ticketing students as young as 6," Yahoo! News, January 10, 2011, https://news.yahoo.com/blogs/lookout/students-young-six-ticketed-police-texas-schools-20110110-083345-614.html.

3. John Dewey, *Impressions of Soviet Russia and the Revolutionary World* (New York: New Republic, Inc., 1929), 57.

4. Jo Ann Boydston, ed., *John Dewey: The Later Works, 1925-1953* (Carbondale: Southern Illinois University Press, 1986), 209.

5. Jo Ann Boydston, ed., *John Dewey: The Middle Works, 1899-1924* (Carbondale: Southern Illinois University Press, 1977), 272.

6. Dewey, *Impressions of Soviet Russia*, 72.

7. Johann Gottlieb Fichte, *Addresses to the German Nation* (Chicago: The Open Court Publishing Co., 1922), 22.

8. Ibid., 187.

UNSAFE SCHOOLS

1. "Robb Elementary School shooting," Wikipedia, accessed November 25, 2022, https://en.wikipedia.org/wiki/Robb_Elementary_School_shooting.

2. Ibid.

3. "Another School Shooting in a Place where teachers and staff were banned from carrying guns: Robb Elementary School in the Uvalde, Texas CISD," Crime Prevention Research Center, May 24, 2022, https://crimeresearch.org/2022/05/another-school-shooting-in-a-place-where-teachers-and-staff-were-

banned-from-carrying-guns-robb-elementary-school-in-the-uvalde-texas-cisd/.

4. "GKA—Community Relations: Conduct on School Premises," Uvalde CISD Board Policy Manual, accessed November 25, 2022, https://pol.tasb.org/PolicyOnline/PolicyDetails?key=1177&code=GKA.

5. "A Brief History of School Violence in the United States," Verso Books, March 23, 2018, https://www.versobooks.com/blogs/3705-a-brief-history-of-school-violence-in-the-united-states-2011.

6. Ibid.

7. "Crime, Violence, Discipline, and Safety in U.S. Public Schools in 2019–20," Institute of Education Sciences, July 2022, https://nces.ed.gov/pubs2022//2022029Summary.pdf.

8. Ibid.

9. "A Brief History..."

DUMBED DOWN CURRICULUM

1. "The Fall and Rise of the 8th Grade School," Bank Street School for Children, accessed November 25, 2022, https://school.bankstreet.edu/about/our-approach/progressive-education-rooted-in-tradition/the-fall-and-rise-of-the-8th-grade-school/.

2. "An 1895 8th Grade Final Exam: I Couldn't Pass It. Could You?," The New Republic, November 27, 2010, https://newrepublic.com/article/79470/1895-8th-grade-final-exam-i-couldnt-pass-it-could-you.

3. Ibid.

4. Ibid.

5. Ibid.

6.   "Century-old 8th-grade exam: Can you pass a 1912 test?," *The Washington Post*, January 15, 2012, https://www.washingtonpost.com/blogs/answer-sheet/post/century-old-8th-grade-exam-can-you-pass-a-1912-test/2012/01/04/gIQAxjC00P_blog.html.

7.   Ibid.

8.   "Bush Warns Against the 'Soft Bigotry Of Low Expectations'," EducationWeek, September 22, 1999, https://www.edweek.org/education/bush-warns-against-the-soft-bigotry-of-low-expecta-tions/1999/09.

9.   "What questions are students able to answer?," The Nation's Report Card, accessed November 25, 2022, https://www.nationsreportcard.gov/reading_math_2013/#/sample-questions.

10. Ibid.

11. Ibid.

12. H.L. Mencken, "The Library," *The American Mercury, vol. 1* (University of California, 1924), 504.

A TOXIC ENVIRONMENT

1.   *Smith v. Guilford Board of Education*, Civil Action No. 3:03-CV-1829 (WWE) (D. Conn. Nov. 30, 2005).

2.   "Guilford family loses lawsuit on bullying," *New Haven Register*, January 7, 2006, https://www.nhregister.com/news/article/Guilford-family-los-es-lawsuit-on-bullying-11643943.php.

3.   Ibid.

4.   Ibid.

5.   "K-12 Education: Students' Experiences with Bul-lying, Hate Speech, Hate Crimes, and Victimiza-

tion in Schools," U.S. Government Accountability Office, November 24, 2021, https://www.gao.gov/products/gao-22-104341.

6. Kathleen Conn, "Bullying in K-12 Public Schools: Searching for Solutions," accessed November 25, 2022, https://cepi.vcu.edu/media/cepi/pdfs/bullying.pdf.

7. "K-12 Education: Students' Experiences with Bullying, Hate Speech, Hate Crimes, and Victimization in Schools."

8. "Summary of Our Cyberbullying Research (2007-2021)," Cyberbullying Research Center, June 22, 2022, https://cyberbullying.org/summary-of-our-cyberbullying-research.

9. Conn, "Bullying in K-12 Public Schools: Searching for Solutions."

10. Ibid.

11. "I Decided to Homeschool Because of Bullying in School," Time4Learning, May 30, 2019, https://www.time4learning.com/blog/homeschool/i-decided-to-homeschool-because-of-bullying-in-school/.

A LINEAR MODEL

1. Kevin Hillstrom and Laurie Collier Hillstrom, eds., *Industrial Revolution in America: Automobiles* (Santa Barbara: ABC-CLIO, 2006), 90.

2. Ibid., 88.

3. Ibid.

4. Ibid.

5. Ibid.

6. Jeannie Oakes and Martin Lipton, *Making the Best of Schools: A Handbook for Parents, Teachers, and*

Policymakers (New Haven: Yale University Press, 1991), 167.

7.   Cynthia McAllister, *A Pedagogical Design for Human Flourishing: Transforming Schools with the McCallister Model* (New York: Routledge, 2022), 25.

8.   Ibid.

POOR PROBLEM SOLVING

1.   David K. Cohen and Penelope L. Peterson, *Effects of State-level Reform of Elementary School Mathematics Curriculum on Classroom Practice* (East Lansing: The National Center for Research on Teacher Education, 1990), 129.

2.   "I'm a high school teacher.," EgoDefenseMechanism, Reddit, accessed November 26, 2022, https://www.reddit.com/r/Professors/comments/hrf999/comment/fy4v36p/; emphasis added.

3.   "Standardized Achievement Tests: What Are They Good For? Hint: Not Cognitive Ability.," Scientific American, December 20, 2013, https://blogs.scientificamerican.com/beautiful-minds/standardized-achievement-tests-what-are-they-good-for-hint-not-cognitive-ability/.

4.   *Occupational Education Forum, vol. 18-20* (Pennsylvania State University, 1989), 2.

5.   Celia B. Fisher and Richard M. Lerner, eds., *Encyclopedia of Applied Developmental Science, vol. 1* (Thousand Oaks: Sage Publications, 2005), 878.

6.   Clifford H. Edwards, *Educational Change: From Traditional Education to Learning Communities* (New York: Rowman & Littlefield Publishers, 2011), 10.

CHASING THE WRONG GOALS

1. "Why conventional education is failing us – Interview with valedictorian Erica Goldson," The Uncommon Life, November 15, 2010, http://www.theuncommonlife.com/blog/conventional-education-failing-us-interview-erica-goldson/.

COMPETITION OVER COLLABORATION

1. "'I Cheated All Throughout High School'," The Atlantic, December 24, 2013, https://www.theatlantic.com/education/archive/2013/12/i-cheated-all-throughout-high-school/282566/.
2. Ibid.
3. Ibid.
4. Ibid.
5. "Why Students Cheat—and What to Do About It," Edutopia, April 27, 2018, https://www.edutopia.org/article/why-students-cheat-and-what-do-about-it.

NOT "COLLEGE READY"

1. "In college remedial classes, unprepared students get the least-trained teachers," The Hechinger Report, March 8, 2016, https://hechingerreport.org/who-helps-those-who-need-help-most/.
2. "Addressing the needs of under-prepared students in Higher Education: Does college remediation work?," *Journal of Human Resources*, 44(3), 736-771.
3. "Most colleges enroll students who aren't prepared for higher education," PBS, January 30,

2017, https://www.pbs.org/newshour/education/colleges-enroll-students-arent-prepared-higher-education.

4.   Ibid.

5.   "Alabama Remedial Education: One-Third of Students Unprepared for College," *Huffington Post*, July 13, 2011, https://www.huffpost.com/entry/alabama-remedial-educatio_n_897167.

6.   "Most colleges enroll students who aren't prepared for higher education."

7.   "College students increasingly caught in remedial education trap," The Hechinger Report, July 2, 2018, https://hechingerreport.org/college-students-increasingly-caught-in-remedial-education-trap/.

8.   "How To Fix America's College Remediation Issue," *U.S. News and World Report*, July 3, 2014, https://www.usnews.com/news/articles/2014/07/03/schools-and-colleges-still-struggle-to-reduce-the-need-for-remedial-education.

9.   Ibid.

10.   "College And Career Readiness Is A Snare And A Delusion," *Forbes*, February 18, 2021, https://www.forbes.com/sites/petergreene/2021/02/18/college-and-career-readiness-is-a-snare-and-a-delusion/?sh=58b73f941b59.

11.   Ibid.

12.   "Alabama Remedial Education: One-Third of Students Unprepared for College."

JUST-IN-CASE LEARNING

1.   "Item 5. The Origins of Just-in-Time," Toyota, accessed December 1, 2022, https://www.toyota-

global.com/company/history_of_toyota/75years/
text/taking_on_the_automotive_business/chap-
ter2/section4/item5.html.

COMPULSION

1. "The Twelve-Year Sentence: The 'Historical Origins' of Compulsory Schooling," Libertarianism.org,
January 1, 1974, https://www.libertarianism.org/
publications/essays/twelve-year-sentence-histori-
cal-origins-compulsory-schooling.
2. Ibid.
3. Ibid.
4. Ibid.
5. "Throwback Thursday: Massachusetts Passes
the Nation's First Compulsory Education Law,"
Boston Magazine, May 17, 2018, https://www.
bostonmagazine.com/education/2018/05/17/
tbt-compulsory-education-massachusetts/.
6. "Why is School Mandatory?," Foundation for Economic Education, June 29, 2016, https://fee.org/
articles/why-is-school-compulsory/.
7. "Oregon Compulsory Education Act," Wikipedia,
accessed December 3, 2022, https://en.wikipedia.
org/wiki/Oregon_Compulsory_Education_Act.
8. Ibid.
9. Ibid.

UNIONIZED MEDIOCRITY

1. "Why Teachers Unions are the Worst of the
Worst," California Policy Center, August 1,
2018, https://californiapolicycenter.org/
why-teachers-unions-are-the-worst-of-the-worst/.

2. "Letter on the Resolution of Federation of Federal Employees Against Strikes in Federal Service," The American Presidency Project, accessed December 3, 2022, https://www.presidency.ucsb.edu/documents/letter-the-resolution-federation-federal-employees-against-strikes-federal-service.

3. "The Case Against Public Sector Unions," Hoover Institution, August 1, 2010, https://www.hoover.org/research/case-against-public-sector-unions.

DIVERSE DISAGREEMENT

1. "Bullis Mountain View is a Wonderful Opportunity For Us," Mountain View Voice, December 17, 2018, https://www.mv-voice.com/square/2018/12/17/bullis-mountain-view-is-a-wonderful-opportunity-for-us.

2. Ibid.

3. Ibid.

4. "Census Bureau Reports Nearly 77 Million Students Enrolled in U.S. Schools," United States Census Bureau, December 3, 2019, https://www.census.gov/newsroom/press-releases/2019/school-enrollment.html.

5. "Barrington parents demand answers about changes to high school's curriculum," MSN, accessed December 3, 2022, https://www.msn.com/en-us/news/us/barrington-parents-demand-answers-about-changes-to-high-school-s-curriculum/ar-AAVo2pN.

6. Ibid.

7. "Despite what you hear, parents aren't in charge of schools. That's a good thing.," USA Today, October 23, 2022, https://www.usatoday.com/story/

opinion/columnist/2022/10/23/public-schools-parents-book-bans-lgbtq-studies-critical-race-theory/10562451002/.

8.   Ibid.

NOT GOOD ENOUGH FOR THE ELITE

1.   "The Powerful Parent Network Is in Pittsburgh and They're Asking Democratic Candidates to Meet With Them," Citizen Ed, December 14, 2019, https://citizen.education/2019/12/14/the-powerful-parent-network-is-in-pittsburgh-and-theyre-asking-democratic-candidates-to-meet-with-them/.

2.   Public Support Grows for Higher Teacher Pay and Expanded School Choice," *Education Next*, vol. 20, no. 1, https://www.educationnext.org/school-choice-trump-era-results-2019-education-next-poll/.

3.   "Liz Warren's latest lie only deepens her dilemma on education," *New York Post*, November 26, 2019, https://nypost.com/2019/11/26/liz-warrens-latest-lie-only-deepens-her-dilemma-on-education/.

4.   "Academic Performance," Council for American Private Education, accessed December 4, 2022, https://capenetwork.org/academic-performance/.

5.   "School Choice and a Lesson in Hypocrisy," The Heritage Foundation, April 21, 2009, https://www.heritage.org/education/commentary/school-choice-and-lesson-hypocrisy.

LOOKING TO THE PAST, NOT FUTURE

1.   "Are Schools Failing Kids in 21st Century Skills?," The Journal, November 14, 2007, https://thejour-

nal.com/articles/2007/11/14/are-schools-failing-kids-in-21st-century-skills.aspx.

2.   "Can K-12 Education Prepare Students For 'Jobs of the Future?'," EducationWeek, May 4, 2017, https://www.edweek.org/leadership/can-k-12-education-prepare-students-for-jobs-of-the-future/2017/05.

3.   Clifford H. Edwards, *Educational Change: From Traditional Education to Learning Communities* (New York: Rowman & Littlefield Publishers, Inc.), 2011.

LOCAL LACK OF CONTROL

1.   Martin Blumenson and Kevin Hymel, *Patton: Legendary Commander* (Washington, D.C.: Potomac Books, Inc, 2008), 78.

2.   Ibid.

3.   "Why Putting Your Kids In Public Schools Is Now More Dangerous Than Ever," The Federalist, September 26, 2018, https://thefederalist.com/2018/09/26/putting-kids-public-schools-now-dangerous-ever/.

STUNTING THE GIFTED

1.   "How a top school district tried to block a very gifted child," *The Washington Post*, July 31, 2016, https://www.washingtonpost.com/local/education/how-a-top-school-district-tried-to-block-a-very-gifted-child/2016/07/31/32dfc37a-5513-11e6-bbf5-957ad17b4385_story.html.

2.   Ibid.

3.   Ibid.

4.   Ibid.

5. "How Gifted Children Are Held Back: Unmet Needs And The Limits Of Educating The Top 0.01%," Medical Daily, January 7, 2014, https://www.medicaldaily.com/how-gifted-children-are-held-back-unmet-needs-and-limits-educating-top-001-266538.

6. Ibid.

7. Ibid.

8. "Back to school: Are we leaving gifted students behind?," *The Christian Science Monitor*, August 31, 2011, https://news.yahoo.com/back-school-leaving-gifted-students-behind-174300508.html.

9. Ibid.

10. Ibid.

11. Ibid.

12. "In the Name of Equity, California Will Discourage Students Who Are Gifted at Math," Reason, May 4, 2021, https://reason.com/2021/05/04/california-math-framework-woke-equity-calculus/.

13. "Socialism is the philosophy of failure…," The Churchill Project, Hillsdale College, July 30, 2015, https://winstonchurchill.hillsdale.edu/socialism-is-the-philosophy-of-failure-winston-churchill/.

MEDICATING THE YOUNG, SECRETLY

1. "EXCLUSIVE: Connecticut school nurse, 77, is suspended over 'transphobic' Facebook post revealing that student, 11, was on puberty blockers, 12 others were non-binary, and that teachers were helping some keep it secret," Daily Mail, March 29, 2022, https://www.dailymail.co.uk/news/article-10665389/School-nurse-suspended-revealing-student-11-puberty-blockers.html.

2. Ibid.

3. "Connecticut School Nurse Suspended over Facebook Comments Claiming District Hides Children's Gender Issues from Parents," *The Tennessee Star*, March 31, 2022, https://tennesseestar.com/2022/03/31/connecticut-school-nurse-suspended-over-facebook-comments-claiming-district-hides-childrens-gender-issues-from-parents/.

4. "Accountability Keeps Losing to Public Schooling's Secrecy," *The Connecticut Examiner*, September 27, 2022, https://ctexaminer.com/2022/09/27/accountability-keeps-losing-to-public-schoolings-secrecy/.

5. "Hartford schools in cover-up on gender dysphoria issue," *Journal Inquirer*, April 11, 2022, https://www.journalinquirer.com/opinion/chris_powell/hartford-schools-in-cover-up-on-gender-dysphoria-issue/article_f37a8db4-b939-11ec-8fc0-c3c9c7f09456.html.

6. "'Where The Need Is': Tackling Teen Pregnancy With A Midwife At School," NPR, June 11, 2018, https://www.npr.org/sections/health-shots/2018/06/11/618872842/where-the-need-is-tackling-teen-pregnancy-with-a-midwife-at-school.

7. Ibid.

8. "NYC schools give out morning-after pills to students—without telling parents," *The New York Post*, September 23, 2012, https://nypost.com/2012/09/23/nyc-schools-give-out-morning-after-pills-to-students-without-telling-parents/.

TOO BIG TO FAIL

1. "Bailout critics say they're losing," Politico, September 24, 2008, https://

www.politico.com/story/2008/09/
bailout-critics-say-theyre-losing-013809.

2. "Average Public School Student Size," Public School Review, accessed December 9, 2022, https://www.publicschoolreview.com/average-school-size-stats/national-data.

3. "The Case for Smaller Classes," Harvard Magazine, August 28, 2019, https://www.harvardmagazine.com/2019/08/case-for-smaller-classes.

4. "Class Sizes Set to Shrink in New York City Schools, but at What Cost?," *The New York Times*, June 3, 2022, https://www.nytimes.com/2022/06/03/nyregion/nyc-schools-class-sizes.html.

5. "When Schools Overlook Introverts," *The Atlantic*, September 28, 2015, https://www.theatlantic.com/education/archive/2015/09/introverts-at-school-overlook/407467/.

6. Ibid.

CLASSROOM MISMANAGEMENT

1. "Another new teacher struggling with class-room management and looking for help," Reddit, accessed December 9, 2022, https://www.reddit.com/r/Teachers/comments/pyb097/another_new_teacher_struggling_with_classroom/.

2. Ibid.

3. ReaderofHarlaw, "Classroom management...," Reddit, accessed December 9, 2022, https://www.reddit.com/r/Teachers/comments/u77nz6/comment/i5e3ats/.

4. Automatic_Randomizer, "You are a pretty smug fel-low...," Reddit, accessed December 9, 2022, https://

www.reddit.com/r/Teachers/comments/u77nz6/comment/i5g3dtz/.

5. umKatorMissKath, "I've never worked in high school…," Reddit, accessed December 9, 2022, https://www.reddit.com/r/Teachers/comments/u77nz6/comment/i5dr7u9/.

6. "Classroom Management," National Education Association, accessed December 9, 2022, https://www.nea.org/professional-excellence/student-engagement/classroom-management.

7. "Hey, New Teachers, It's OK To Cry In Your Car," NPR, October 22, 2015, https://www.npr.org/sections/ed/2015/10/22/450575463/it-s-okay-to-cry-in-your-car-fighting-disillusionment-as-a-first-year-teacher.

8. Ibid.

9. "Why Is Classroom Management Such a Problem for New Teachers?," EducationWeek, January 5, 2016, https://www.edweek.org/leadership/why-is-classroom-management-such-a-problem-for-new-teachers/2016/01.

10. "Effective Classroom Management: Teacher Preparation and Professional Development," National Comprehensive Center for Teacher Quality, December 2007, https://files.eric.ed.gov/fulltext/ED543769.pdf.

11. "The First Year of Teaching Can Feel Like a Fraternity Hazing," *The Atlantic*, April 13, 2016, https://www.theatlantic.com/education/archive/2016/04/first-year-teaching/477990/.

12. "The Private School Penalty," Education Rickshaw, March 16, 2022, https://educationrickshaw.com/2022/03/16/the-private-school-penalty/.

13. Ibid.; this is only a partial selection from the list provided.

MONOPOLY

1. "How did Google get so big?," CBS News, May 21, 2018, https://www.cbsnews.com/news/how-did-google-get-so-big/.
2. Ibid.
3. "Google's Search Dominance," Statista, October 21, 2020, https://www.statista.com/chart/23250/search-market-share-in-the-united-states/.

CONCLUSION

1. John Taylor Gatto, *Dumbing Us Down: The Hidden Curriculum of Compulsory Schooling* (Canada: New Society Publishers, 2005), 19.
2. "I Quit, I Think," *The Wall Street Journal*, July 25, 1991.
3. Bill Steigerwald, "John Taylor Gatto: Unlikely Guerrilla," Substack, December 13, 2021, https://clips.substack.com/p/john-taylor-gatto-subversive.
4. Ibid.
5. John Taylor Gatto, "Why Schools Don't Educate," The Natural Child Project, accessed December 22, 2022, https://www.naturalchild.org/articles/guest/john_gatto.html.

Connor Boyack is the founder and president of Libertas Institute, a free-market think tank in Utah. In that capacity, he has spearheaded dozens of successful policy reforms in areas such as education reform, medical freedom, civil liberties, government transparency, entrepreneurship, business  deregulation, personal freedom, and more. Several of these legal changes were the first of their kind in the country, and Libertas Institute has received numerous awards for their innovative work.

A public speaker and author of over 40 books, Connor is best known for *The Tuttle Twins* books, a children's series introducing young readers to economic, political, and civic principles; over five million copies of the books have been sold. He is also executive producer of *The Tuttle Twins*, an animated cartoon series based on the books.

Connor lives near Salt Lake City, Utah, with his wife and two children. Learn more at ConnorBoyack.com.

Corey DeAngelis is a senior fellow at the American Federation for Children. He is also the executive director at Educational Freedom Institute, an adjunct scholar at the Cato Institute, a senior fellow at Reason Foundation, and a board member at Liberty Justice Center. He was named on the Forbes  30 under 30 list for his work on education policy and received the Buckley Award from America's Future in 2020.

DeAngelis has authored or coauthored over 40 journal articles, book chapters, and reports on education policy, and he is the coeditor of *School Choice Myths: Setting the Record Straight on Education Freedom.* His research has been published in peer-reviewed academic journals, including *Social Science Quarterly, School Effectiveness and School Improvement, Educational Review,* and *Peabody Journal of Education.*

DeAngelis received his PhD in education policy from the University of Arkansas. He holds a BBA and an MA in economics from the University of Texas at San Antonio.